AF400788

FACTOLOGY
CASTLES

Open up a world of information!

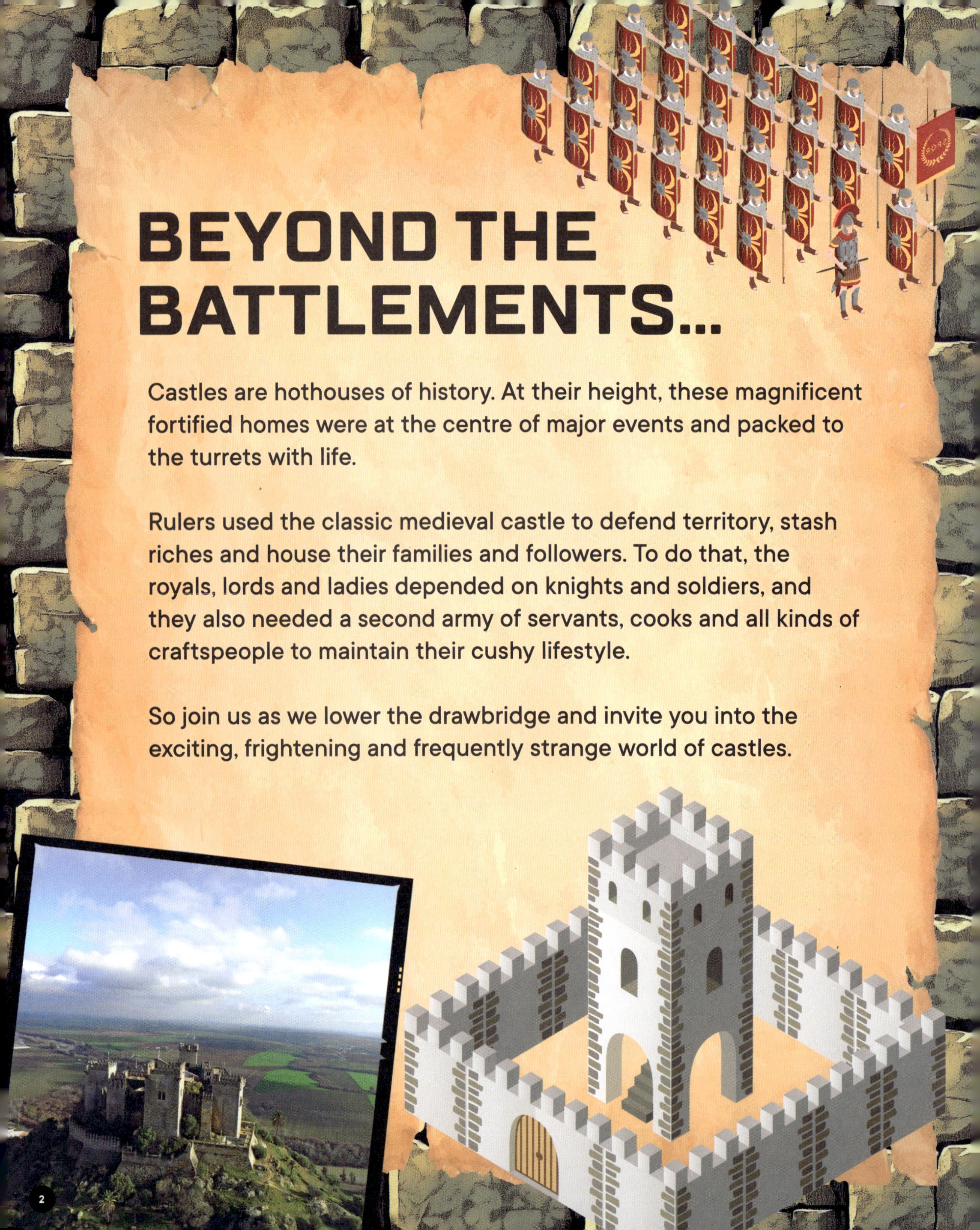

BEYOND THE BATTLEMENTS...

Castles are hothouses of history. At their height, these magnificent fortified homes were at the centre of major events and packed to the turrets with life.

Rulers used the classic medieval castle to defend territory, stash riches and house their families and followers. To do that, the royals, lords and ladies depended on knights and soldiers, and they also needed a second army of servants, cooks and all kinds of craftspeople to maintain their cushy lifestyle.

So join us as we lower the drawbridge and invite you into the exciting, frightening and frequently strange world of castles.

CHAPTER 1
HISTORY OF THE CASTLE

6 What is a castle?
8 Early versions
12 400 years of castles
18 Henry's seaside castles

CHAPTER 2
THE CLASSIC CASTLE

22 Parts of the medieval castle
28 Grand designs
32 The Great Hall
34 The kitchen
36 Castles as prisons

CHAPTER 3
CASTLE LIFE

40 In the name of the lord
42 First ladies
44 Kids in the castle
46 Knights
50 Trusty steeds
52 People of the castle
56 Home comforts
60 A typical day
62 Food & drink
64 Did somebody say... just eat?
66 What they wore
70 Knight games
72 Badge of honour
74 Under siege!

CHAPTER 4
EXTRAORDINARY CASTLES

80 Windsor Castle
84 Escape from Colditz
86 Where is Dracula's castle?
88 Most haunted
92 A 21st-century medieval adventure
94 Glossary
96 Index

CHAPTER 1

HISTORY OF THE CASTLE

Who built the earliest versions, how castles changed over four centuries, and why Henry VIII brought them back to life

WHAT IS A CASTLE?

A castle is the fortified home (sometimes called a stronghold) of a ruler or noble built in medieval times. The word is sometimes also used for grand houses built later in the same style

A VERY QUICK HISTORY OF CASTLES

146 BCE–476 CE

The Romans establish towns all over their Empire. These settlements include forts from where they defend their territory.

534–698

Byzantine Greeks build structures similar to castles during military campaigns in North Africa.

711
From around this date onwards, Muslims build hundreds of forts on hilltops in Spain.

800

Vikings invade Europe, and the first true castles – a fort in which a ruler lives – are built in Western Europe (but not England) to resist them.

1066

Normans invade England and begin building castles. These are simple towers surrounded by a wooden fence.

1080

The first stone castle towers, or keeps, are built around this time.

1150

Inspired by castles in the Middle East, a golden period of building begins in England, France and Germany.

1200

Keeps are now built in different shapes. Rounded keeps are common because they are harder to attack.

1240

Designs include bedrooms and halls for feasts and celebrations.

1280

Stronger castles now include tall inner walls and lower outer walls. Archers fire from the top of these walls.

1350

Castles are now more homes than forts with comforts such as fireplaces, toilets, stone carvings and wider windows.

1400
Cannons can now destroy walls, but some large castles are still built and maintained to look formidable to invading armies.

1540

Traditional castles are vulnerable to cannonballs, but some smaller forts are built with extra thick walls from which to fire cannons.

1642–51

During the English Civil War, castles are used, and some are demolished to stop them being used.

1800s

By now, castles are no longer places where rulers hide from attacks, but a few rich people hoping to impress the neighbours continue to build them.

EARLY VERSIONS

Castles began as wooden buildings on a hill centuries before they grew up to be glorious royal fortresses

IRON AGE BASICS

Maiden Castle in Dorset dates back to around 800 BCE. Hundreds of people are said to have lived there in an area the size of 50 football pitches.

Like other Iron Age fortresses, Maiden Castle was pretty basic. A ditch was dug around a wooden building on a hill and mounds of earth, known as **ramparts**, were piled up around the hill. It was hoped the ramparts and stones fired from slings would put off any attackers.

Unsurprisingly, none of that worked on the mighty Romans when they invaded in 43 CE. With their fancy iron-tipped arrows, they easily defeated the Brits.

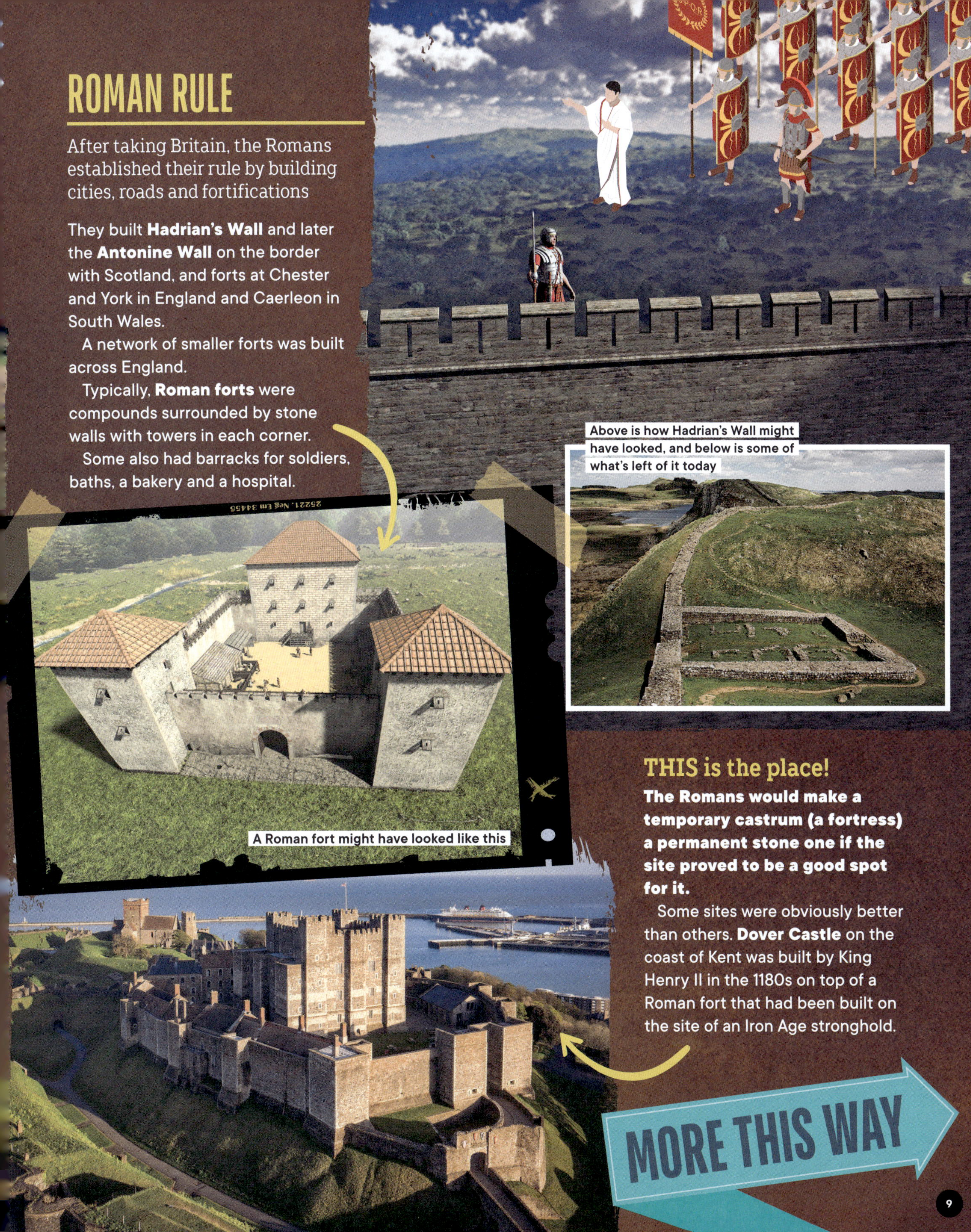

ROMAN RULE

After taking Britain, the Romans established their rule by building cities, roads and fortifications

They built **Hadrian's Wall** and later the **Antonine Wall** on the border with Scotland, and forts at Chester and York in England and Caerleon in South Wales.

A network of smaller forts was built across England.

Typically, **Roman forts** were compounds surrounded by stone walls with towers in each corner.

Some also had barracks for soldiers, baths, a bakery and a hospital.

Above is how Hadrian's Wall might have looked, and below is some of what's left of it today

A Roman fort might have looked like this

THIS is the place!

The Romans would make a temporary castrum (a fortress) a permanent stone one if the site proved to be a good spot for it.

Some sites were obviously better than others. **Dover Castle** on the coast of Kent was built by King Henry II in the 1180s on top of a Roman fort that had been built on the site of an Iron Age stronghold.

THE MYTH OF YOUNG MERLIN

In 410 CE, the Romans left Britain because their troops were needed to fight wars in Germany and Persia, and defend their capital city, Rome.

King Vortigern was then the most powerful man in Britain, but he lived to regret asking the ruthless Saxons of Germany to protect him from the Scots and the Picts.

Vortigern was forced to flee to Wales where, in Gwynedd, he built **Dinas Emrys fort**. Unfortunately, while it was being built, the fort's tower kept falling down.

According to legend, a wise old man told the king that to strengthen the tower he must mix the blood of an innocent, fatherless boy into the cement!

Vortigern offered the old man a boy called **Merlin**, who would grow up to be the magician at the court of King Arthur.

Merlin said that the reason the tower wouldn't stay up was that every night a red dragon fought a white dragon in a pool beneath the site of the castle.

Vortigern decided that the red dragon represented Wales, and the white one was Saxony, so instead of sacrificing Merlin, all he had to do was defeat the Saxons!

And that's said to be one reason why there's a red dragon on the Welsh flag.

Golden boy

It's believed Merlin buried a cauldron of gold beneath Dinas Emrys. It was left there for a special young person with fair hair and blue eyes...

Meanwhile, in Africa...

Armies fighting for the Byzantine empire in North Africa during the 6th century built forts that were similar to what we would recognise as castles today.

Aïn Tounga in modern-day Tunisia had thick stone walls with towers at its corners.

One of the towers was a garrison where soldiers lived and looked like what would later be called a keep.

And in Spain...

Beginning in the 8th century, Muslim rulers (known as Moors) constructed hundreds of forts across the hilltops of Spain.

Castillo de Almodóvar in Córdoba dates to 760 CE and was built on the site of a Roman fort.

Later, it became the residence of the Spanish king Peter the Cruel (1334–69).

9th & 10th CENTURY

WHY THEN?

The **Carolingian Empire** covered territory in what is now France, Germany, Italy and Spain. Civil war tore the empire apart and after it fell in 880 CE, it was divided between its royals and lords.

* These nobles built castles as **symbols of power** and places from which to **rule**, **control trade** and **defend their territory**.

* Countryside castles were often built near **mills**, good **farming land** and sources of **water**.

* In the 9th and 10th centuries, castles were often just **wooden watch towers** built on a hill and surrounded by a wooden fence or palisade.

The Northmen are coming!

Between the 9th and 11th centuries, seafaring warriors from Scandinavia attacked Western European countries.

These Northmen or **Vikings** made many raids on the north coast of France. In 911, King Rollo claimed the French territory we now know as Normandy for the Vikings.

The Vikings who settled in Normandy became known as Normans, and the kings that came after Rollo became more and more powerful and ambitious.

In 1066, **William the Conqueror** and his forces invaded England and defeated King Harold's army at the **Battle of Hastings**.

Meanwhile, in Britain...

There were no proper roads or cities in 9th-and 10th-century Britain. It was mainly forests, farmlands, villages, a few towns and the odd castle

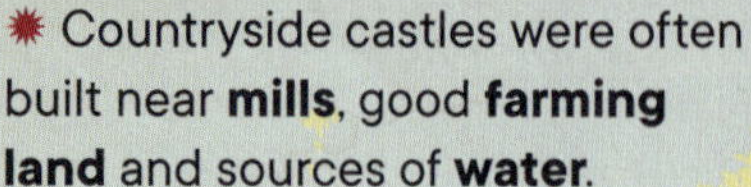

11th CENTURY

CONQUERED!

England didn't have many castles. It's estimated that the kingdom had as few as six in 1066.

✳ That meant that when he went to battle, Harold risked everything, including his throne, because, unlike other kings, he did not have the backing of a series of strongholds throughout his kingdom.

✳ After winning the Battle of Hastings, the Normans faced very little resistance when taking over England.

FLAT PACK!

The **Normans** built their first castle in England at Hastings. Hundreds of years before IKEA thought of it, they **brought the pieces with them** and put the castle together on the site.

Show-offs!

The Normans built castles with high towers. There was no obvious military reason for this, it was just them showing off and using their castles as symbols of power.

Built around 1127, **Rochester Castle** in Kent has three floors, stands 34.5-metres high and has the tallest surviving Norman keep.

William divided England between his knights, and they forced local people to help build their castles for them. Rebellions were common, and in response troops would quash the uprising and a castle would be built near the rebellious town.

✳ Thirty-four years after the Normans arrived, at the end of the 11th century, it's estimated there were more than 500 British castles!

✳ Merchants and craftsmen would settle near a lord's castle, offer him their services and a town or city would then develop.

✳ Examples of this are Ghent, Ypres and Bruges in Belgium and Newcastle upon Tyne in England (the clue's in the name!).

500 CASTLES IN THE UK
BY END OF 11TH CENTURY

MOTTE & BAILEY

A 'motte' was the mound of earth that the castle's keep (tower) sat on. A 'bailey' was the courtyard between the motte and the wooden fence (palisade) that surrounded the castle.

✳ This style of timber castle was quite cheap and very quick to build.

✳ The first motte-and-bailey castles are thought to have appeared during the late 10th century.

✳ Starting in the early 11th century, the Normans built hundreds of them.

✳ It'll be no surprise to hear that the original wooden motte-and-bailey castles no longer exist, but you can see a very cool reconstruction of one in Saint-Sylvain-d'Anjou in France.

MOTTE The mound would typically be 30 to 92 metres across and 3 to 30 metres high. It could be a natural hill or a huge pile of soil.

BAILEY The garrison where the lord's soldiers lived would be in the bailey. Larger castles might have two or three baileys in front of the motte. The **kitchen**, **smithy**, **stables**, **servant's quarters**, **stores** and **barns** were all in the bailey.

ADDED EXTRAS

At the beginning of the 1100s, most castles were still made of wood. Many would be converted to stone over the next 100 years as their lords got richer through taxes, tolls and rent.

✳ The motte-and-bailey castles were now **shell keeps**. That means the timber wall around the tower was replaced by a stone wall.

✳ Occasionally, if the **motte was too soft to support the stone keep**, then it would have to be built below on the bailey.

✳ **Keeps were now usually rectangular** rather than round, and often built on naturally high or rocky ground.

✳ The shell keep at **Château de Langeais** in the Loire, France, is believed to date to the 10th century, but they became more common during the 11th and 12th centuries.

✳ A keep could be **18 metres high** or more. The entrance was on the second storey via a stairway inside the keep.

✳ Another layer of defence was a crenellated low stone wall or **parapet**. The Romans built something similar long before the castle-builders.

Great new feature

✳ By the 12th century, as castles got bigger and more impressive, the main room in the keep became the **Great Hall** on the first floor,

✳ The ground floor of the keep was used for storage.

THE CRUSADES

Castle-building was heavily influenced by the Crusades, a series of military campaigns by Western European Christian nations between 1095 and 1291

The Christians wanted to stop the progress of Muslim powers in what's now Turkey and the Middle East. There, Christian armies came up against stone castles that were bigger and grander than anything they had in their homelands.

☀ The English and other Europeans made use of the building techniques of their Greek allies and Turkish enemies.

☀ These new castles featured long walls with towers at regular intervals and sometimes included natural rock faces and cliff edges in their designs.

☀ The Muslims also built more than one castle to defend a single territory. Several local castles could support each other in fighting enemies.

☀ The Crusaders made these features part of their own castles in the Middle East, and were inspired to build larger, more impressive castles back in Europe.

A 1954 painting by Said Tahsin of the surrender of Crusader Guy of Lusignan to Saladin, Sultan of Egypt and Syria

Krak des Chevaliers

Built during the 12th century in what is now Syria, this is thought to be the most impressive of the Crusaders' castles still standing. It has two layers of walls with towers, a wide moat, and its garrison housed around 2,000 soldiers.

Caerphilly Castle, Wales

BEST DEFENCE

✴ Inspired by the fortifications used during the Crusades, 12th-century castles had extra walls.

✴ Inside the outer wall was another wall that connected a series of towers, one of which would be the ruler's home. As these concentric castles became more secure, buildings were expanded and added.

✴ Castles were now often built with the main bailey at the back and lines of defence at the front. **Caerphilly Castle** in South Wales, built between 1267 and 1277 and located on an island in a lake, is a prime example.

✴ The keep might also have its own moat and drawbridge as well as a low wall called a **chemise**.

James the builder

✴ Between 1280 to 1320, the most impressive of Britain's castles were constructed. Many of them were built in Wales by Edward I's favourite engineer, **James of St George**.

✴ In 1283, James began work on the castles at Cowy, Harlech and Caernarfon. He is said to have had around 1,500 men working for him.

✴ These castles were part of what became known as the **Ring of Iron**, a collection of castles built to impose the English crown's control over the rebellious Welsh.

✴ James's style was a square castle with two concentric walls and towers at each corner. There was no keep because towers were thought strong enough to keep out the enemy, even if they managed to get into the bailey.

✴ Natural settings were used as extra defences.

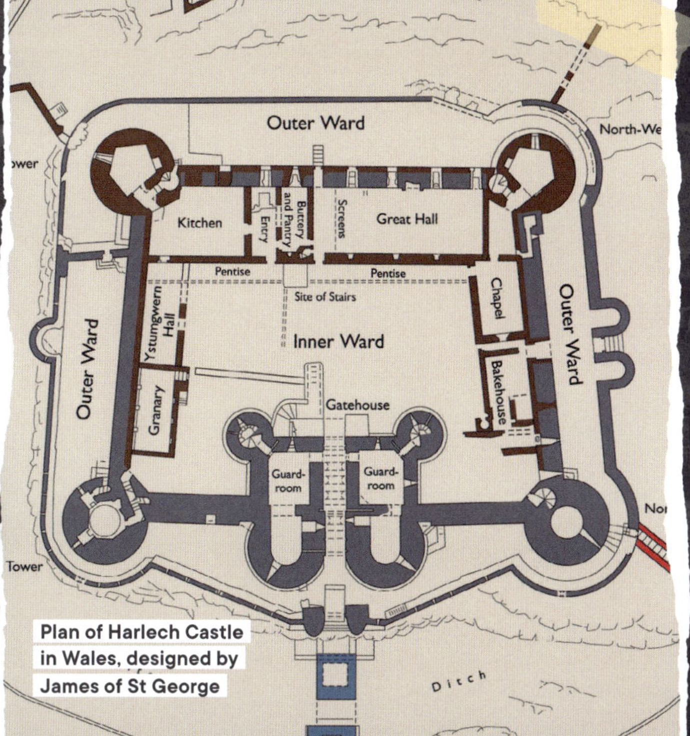

Plan of Harlech Castle in Wales, designed by James of St George

HENRY'S SEASIDE

Why did Henry VIII build castles?

- After breaking away from the Catholic Church so he could dispose of his wives and remarry, Henry feared attacks from Spain and France.

- So, although the golden days of castle-building were long gone, between 1539 and 1547, Henry ordered the construction of a series of 'device forts'.

- Until this time, defence of the coastline had been left to local rulers. 'Device' was another word for the king's plan or instruction.

- They were called castles even though, in reality, they were forts to be defended by soldiers.

- Henry took a close interest in the forts and amended designs to include his own ideas.

- Henry paid for the forts with the treasures he took when he closed his kingdom's monasteries.

30 FORTS finished in the first year of building

6 WAYS TO SPOT ONE OF HENRY'S DEVICE FORTS

1 STONE PARAPETS
Low, thick protective walls that could take the impact of a cannonball.

2 CIRCULAR DESIGN
A round shape meant cannons could defend the castle on all sides.

3 GUN POSITIONS
Built into the inside walls they had their own vents which took away gun smoke.

4 BASTIONS
These were extended sections of the wall, often at the corners of the castle, from which cannons were fired.

5 COAT OF ARMS OVER THE FRONT DOOR
Henry left his mark just in case there was any doubt about who was in charge.

6 TURRETS
Towers with a small room at the top from where a guard could keep a lookout for enemies.

CASTLES

Between 1539 and 1547, King Henry VIII built forts to defend the coasts of England and Wales – but why did he do it?

DEAL WITH IT!

A prime example of a device fort is **Deal Castle** in Kent.

Deal was a major English port at the time and Henry built three castles in the area – the other two were Sandown and Walmer – to defend the beaches of the Kent Downs and the town.

The three were linked by a chain of four earthwork forts and together they were known as the 'Castles of the Downs'.

Around 1,400 men worked on the construction of Deal Castle and lead, wood and stone from local monasteries closed by Henry were recycled in the building.

IN 1540 **Thomas Wingfield** was appointed the **first captain** of the castle. It's reported he commanded eight soldiers, 16 gunners and two porters.

IN 1648 During the **English Civil War**, the castle was seized by Royalists and only taken over by Parliamentarians after a siege that lasted several months.

UNTIL 1904 Deal was maintained for military purposes, but brought back into service as an observation post in **World War II**.

TODAY Deal Castle is a **popular museum** and still has cannons and a captain – but that's all ceremonial now!

What happened next?

Henry VIII expanded his army and navy, and also improved defences in Calais and Guisnes, two French towns that were under his control.

The French attacked the Isle of Wight in 1545, but aside from that the device forts never saw battle with other European powers, before peace was declared in 1546.

FACT DEVICE FORTS ARE ALSO KNOWN AS **HENRICIAN CASTLES**, **ARTILLERY CASTLES** OR **BLOCKHOUSES**

CHAPTER 2

THE CLASSIC CASTLE

A guide to the construction and key parts
of the medieval fortified home in its prime

PARTS OF A MEDIEVAL CASTLE

The bits that make a classic castle a castle, and how they worked

TOWER
CRENEL
MOAT
BATTLEMENT
CURTAIN WALL
MORE THIS WAY

Reconstruction of wooden keep,
Saint-Sylvain-d'Anjou, France

The keep's **spiral staircases were built in a clockwise direction**. This made it difficult for right-handed attackers to use their swords when they climbed the stairs. Clever!

The Norman stone keep at
Hedingham Castle, England

KEEP

As the place where the lord lived, the tower or keep was the most important and best protected part of the castle.

* Because the **wooden towers** of early castles were vulnerable to fire, **shell keeps** had stone walls, sometimes built on top of the motte, to protect the keep.

* Later, the **Normans built stone castles with high towers**. There was no obvious military reason for this, it was just them showing off and using their castles as symbols of power.

THE WELL

This was usually below or near the keep so that if under siege, the lord and family had water. Later, advanced castles had pipes that carried water from the well up two or three storeys of the keep to drawing places on each floor.

The well at Bodiam
Castle, England

CURTAIN WALL

A thick stone wall was built around the keep. These outer walls were thickest at the bottom to protect them from battering rams.

The walls were also often sloped at the bottom. During a siege, large stones dropped from the castle would then bounce off the slope towards approaching enemies.

Arzignano Castle, Italy

The fighting tower (or bergfried) at Lichtenberg Castle, Germany

TOWERS & FIGHTING PLATFORMS

These were places from which archers could shoot at enemies. Early versions were made of timber and later models were built of stone.

Concentric castles

These were castles with another wall surrounding the curtain wall as an extra line of defence. A low wall was known as a **parapet**.

Beaumaris Castle, Wales

MORE THIS WAY

BATTLEMENTS

CRENELS

These are the openings, usually under a metre wide, at the top of the wall through which archers could fire arrows and others could throw things at enemies.

✳ 'Crenulated' is the word for something with an up-and-down outline, like battlements.

MERLONS

The sections of the castle wall – around two to three metres high – between the crenels.

✳ Together with the narrow walkway behind them, they form the battlements.

MACHICOLATION

Sometimes called a 'murder hole', this is a gap in the wall that hangs over the side of the castle.

✳ Stones and boiling water were dropped through these gaps onto attackers below.

ARROW LOOP

The slit in the castle wall through which archers fired arrows. They were narrow to make it difficult to shoot back at the archer.

✳ Inside, the walls either side of the arrow loop were designed to give archers space to stand. Some even had a seat built in.

✳ Arrow loops were also called 'meurtrières', which is French for murderesses!

Trogir Castle, Croatia

GATEHOUSE

At first this was just an opening in a tower – later it was a gate between towers.

To strengthen the defences of the gatehouse, a fortified tower known as a **barbican** might be added. Exeter Castle in Devon, England has an early Norman towered gatehouse.

Exeter Castle, England

Leeds Castle, England

PORTCULLIS

A heavy oak and iron door was another layer of defence. It was moved up and down by a pulley.

MOAT

A trench dug around the castle's outer wall that was often, but not always, filled with water.

Some were left dry and had sharp stakes (spikes) in the bottom as a nasty surprise for enemies. Y'ouch!

When filled with water, moats could get pretty stinky. Human poo and wee often ended up in there, along with horse manure and cow dung!

Caerlaverock Castle, Scotland

DRAWBRIDGE

The gatehouse of a castle with a moat would have a drawbridge.

As you might guess, the bridge could be drawn up for extra protection or lowered to allow people into the castle.

Forte da Ponta da Bandeira, Portugal

GRAND DESIGNS

It could take a huge of team of people years to build a medieval castle. Here's who they were and how they made it happen

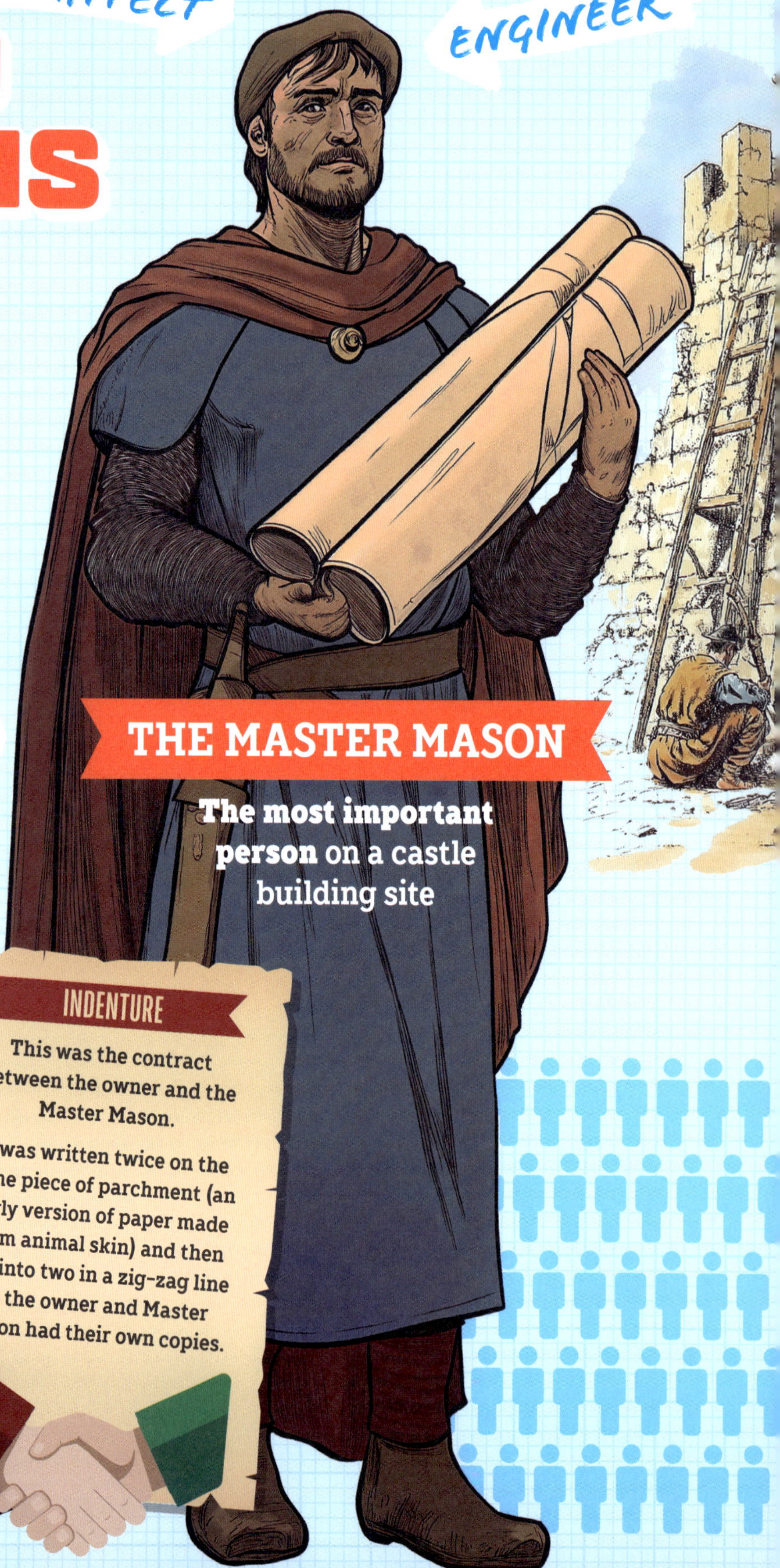

THE BOSS

Before there was such a thing as an architect to design buildings and an engineer to make sure the plans worked, the **Master Mason** did both jobs and more.

He would talk to the castle's owner about what he wanted, and agree on a price and a date when the building would be finished.

THE MASTER MASON

The most important person on a castle building site

The King had to grant a 'licence to crenellate' (in other words, to build a fortified home with battlements) before a castle could be built.

SIGNED:
The King

INDENTURE

This was the contract between the owner and the Master Mason.

It was written twice on the same piece of parchment (an early version of paper made from animal skin) and then cut into two in a zig-zag line so the owner and Master Mason had their own copies.

Trend setters
Experienced craftsmen would travel between building sites across countries, picking up and using different styles and techniques as they went.

An army of builders

Hundreds of people were needed to build a castle. Just one door involved a mason to make the doorway, a carpenter to make the door, a blacksmith to make the lock and hinges, plus a team of men to lift it into place.

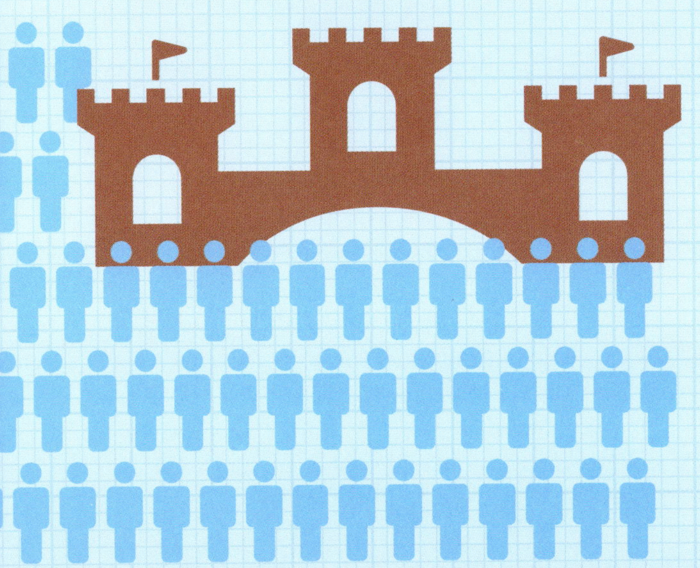

WHO WORKED FOR THE MASTER MASON?

All these craftspeople played crucial roles on the building site

CARPENTER
As well as building the scaffolding, doors, galleries, bridges and shutters, every castle needed a wooden water mill to grind flour.

STONE CUTTER
Stone needed to be cut from the quarry and dressed (made smooth and sculpted into shape).

BLACKSMITH
Not much happened without the blacksmith who made, repaired and sharpened tools, and also made the nails.

ROPEMAKER
Ropes were essential for pulleys and ties used when lifting heavy materials.

TILE MAKER
Handmade tiles were needed for the roof and floors.

☑ *Build a castle*

1 FIND A SITE

Castles were often built on a steep hill, by the coast or on a road – any place that could be defended and was good for trade.

✳ Thousands of tons of soil and stone were needed along with sand, lime and water to make mortar to hold everything together. Clay was used for the floor and roof tiles.

✳ There were no dumper trucks, so all of these materials needed to be near the building site.

✳ Heavy materials would be transported by horse and cart.

✳ Timber for building and fuel for fires and furnaces was needed, so it was handy if there was woodland close by.

2 DIG A DITCH

A ditch or moat was dug around the castle for extra defence, and the soil might be used elsewhere in the building.

3 BUILD WALLS

Before bricks were invented, walls were built with rough stone and mortar. They could be up to 2.4 metres thick, and made up of two layers, with rubble in between.

4 CUT STONES

For the parts of the castle that needed to be smooth and precise – such as floors, windows and staircases – stone blocks (called ashlars) were cut and worked into shapes.

✳ Stone cutters used axes, hammers, wedges and chisels, and cut around wooden templates for accuracy.

Fa'side Castle, Scotland

Paint job

✳ The outside of the castle was often plastered and painted white with quicklime to weatherproof the stone and mortar.

✳ Some house-proud nobles had both the inside and outside of their castles painted in bright colours.

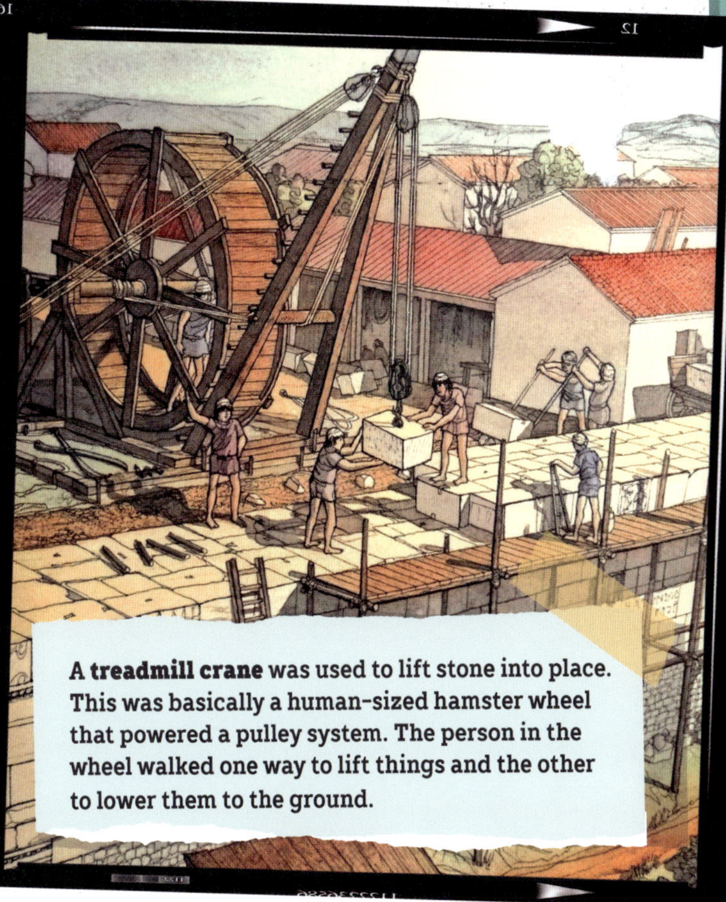

A **treadmill crane** was used to lift stone into place. This was basically a human-sized hamster wheel that powered a pulley system. The person in the wheel walked one way to lift things and the other to lower them to the ground.

Interior of Dover Castle, England

5 MAKE MORTAR

Mortar was what held the stones together. It was made by burning chalk or limestone in an oven. This transformed it into quicklime, which was mixed with water and sand to make mortar.

Fair-weather builders

✳ In England and other Northern European countries, castles were usually only built in spring and summer.

✳ During colder months, the sites were covered to protect them from bad weather. This is probably why they took years to build!

THE GREAT HALL

The Great Hall was on the first floor of a castle's keep. Castle-dwellers had to climb a flight of steps to enter.

The hall would often occupy the entire floor. In early castles, the lord's family slept in the hall behind a curtain or screen.

The hall was heated by a fireplace. There was a hole in its ceiling to let out the smoke from the fire. In early medieval castles, the fire was in the middle of the hall and moved to the wall in later eras. The lord and lady had the seats closest to the fire (naturally!).

The high table

The lord and family sat at the high table. Set up on a platform or **dais**, this was the table furthest away from the door to avoid draughts and being bothered by new arrivals.

Seating

The lord and lady had bigger chairs that were sometimes covered by canopies.

Everyone else sat on benches at long temporary tables that were taken away after meals. All tables were covered with white cloths.

In early castles, the **buttery**, from where drinks (not butter!) were served, and the **pantry**, where bread was stored, were separate wooden huts in the bailey. By the 12th century, they were attached to the hall, as was a latrine (a very basic toilet).

At the heart of every medieval castle was a hall where the lord's family, friends and guests feasted and partied

MEDIEVAL INSTRUMENTS

LIZARD
An S-shaped woodwind instrument

CRUMHORN
A woodwind instrument that looked like an upside-down walking stick

LUTE
This looked like a guitar but was pear-shaped and had a bent neck

HURDY-GURDY
This also looked like a guitar with a handle that was turned to get the strings to make a sound

Instruments still used today, such as **flutes**, **harps** and **bagpipes**, were also played.

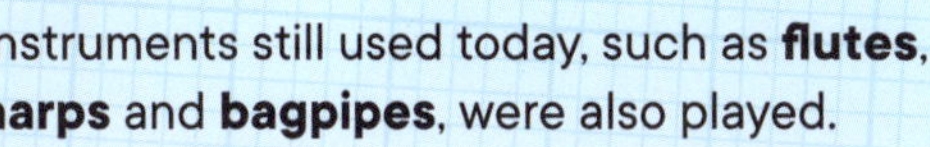

Travelling **minstrels** (singers and musicians), **troubadours** (poets) and **jongleurs** (singers or musicians who also juggled and performed acrobatics) would visit castles to entertain the nobles and their friends.

Windows
These had wooden shutters and were secured by iron bars. Glass was first used for windows in the 13th century and was common by the 14th century.

The first halls had a high ceiling with a timber roof supported by wooden posts or stone pillars. Later, carpenters used a method that didn't need pillars.

English King Henry II had a favourite Jester called **Roland the Musical Farter**. He was such a good fool he was gifted Hemingstone Manor, a big house in Suffolk with 30 acres of land!

Surely, you jest!
✳ **Originally, the word jester meant 'storyteller', but it became the name of a man who played the fool** – telling jokes, dancing and making silly noises.

✳ Jesters were allowed to mock nobles and say things others dare not say – although this was obviously a risky thing to do...

✳ Jesters wore brightly coloured outfits, bells and a hood with donkey's ears and would make audiences laugh with an inflated pig's bladder on a stick.

THE KITCHEN

Busy throughout the day and full of servants of every kind, if the Great Hall was the heart of the castle, the kitchen was its soul

Where was it?

The earliest kitchens in medieval castles were separate from the main buildings but later versions were connected by passageways.

Up until the 13th century, kitchens were often sited away from the keep and built of timber.

Utensils were washed in a separate building called the **scullery**.

Animals were slaughtered for fresh meat nearby.

Temporary **extra kitchens** were set up for major feasts.

It was not common for the kitchen to be in the keep as part of the Great Hall or one of the main buildings until the 15th century.

Near the kitchen in the bailey there was often a **garden** which had fruit trees, grape vines, herbs and flowers. If the castle was particularly fancy it might also have a **fishpond**.

Soups and stews were made in **huge cauldrons**. These were hung over the fire **on a hook and chain and lowered or raised** to adjust the cooking temperature.

Fats from cooking were collected and re-used or **made into candles**.

Larger castles might have their own **baker** and **bakery**.

Sometimes the cauldrons were put in their own room, called the **boiling room**.

The kitchen at Dover Castle as it would have looked in the 12th century

Pots were made of **iron**, **copper** or **bronze** and jugs were made of **pottery**.

HOT STUFF!
Food was cooked over an open fire or in an oven set in the wall.

Meat was cooked on long metal poles or **spits** over a fire. **Boys** were sometimes given the job of **turning the spits** as the meat cooked.

CASTLES AS PRISONS

When you think of a dungeon, a castle's dark, damp underground prison might come to mind, but were they really that common in the medieval era?

TAKE HIM TO THE TOWER!

During the 9th and 10th centuries, prison wasn't often the punishment for breaking the law. It was more common for offenders to be fined.

Few medieval castles had prisons or dungeons, and if they had prisoners, they were more likely to be held in irons and kept in the guardroom of a tower.

Law & order

During the reign of Henry II (1133–89), jails became more common. In 1166, the King ordered his sheriffs to establish a prison in every county and use castles if necessary.

☀ We know that between 1166 and 1230, prisons were set up in 14 royal castles across the country, but we don't have many details of what went on in them.

☀ During the 1170s, Henry had a chamber in the basement of the tower of his castle at Newcastle upon Tyne, which is thought to have been used as a prison.

Caesar's Tower

In Caesar's Tower at Warwick Castle, there is a prison basement (sometimes called an oubliette, from the French word 'oublier', meaning 'to forget') built during the 14th century, and only accessible via the courtyard.

☀ There was a latrine and a window with a grille through which guards could check on prisoners.

☀ In 1455, the Earl of Warwick imprisoned Edward IV here during the Wars of the Roses.

DUNGEONS

Dungeons are often thought of as dark, damp prisons beneath a castle.

✳ But the word 'dungeon' came from 'donjon', the French word for a castle tower, said to be the place criminals were more likely to be imprisoned.

✳ In Scotland, there's evidence of 'pit prisons' or 'bottle dungeons', windowless lower floors of towers accessed via a hatch at the top.

✳ It's thought these were built as dungeons (not converted from other types of room) because they included a toilet or latrine.

✳ There may also have been pit prisons at York, Leicester and Nottingham's royal castles, but dungeons in castles were rare in medieval times.

Class divides

Historians believe that commoners were usually jailed in the dungeon, while the nobles were locked up in a more comfortable room above.
   Castles were the most important buildings, so their prisoners were of a higher status.

In the 13th century, there were three prisons in London…

FLEET
for those who had broken laws of contracts and property

NEWGATE
for serious criminals such as murderers

TOWER OF LONDON
for VIP prisoners

Prisons of the future…

✳ **British castles at Lancaster (above), Chester, Norwich, Lincoln, Leicester and Carmarthen were later adapted into modern prisons.**

✳ **Some 19th century prisons, such as Lewes Prison in Sussex, were designed to look like castles with battlements and gatehouses.**

INMATE MARY

On the orders of Elizabeth I, Mary, Queen of Scots was held for 19 years in locations around the country, including Tutbury, Carlisle, Bolton and Sheffield castles. She lived a life of luxury, and was looked after by servants, before she was executed for treason at Fotheringhay Castle in February 1587.

CHAPTER 3
CASTLE LIFE

How lords and ladies lived their best lives
with help from loyal followers, and what
happened when they were besieged by
their enemies...

IN THE NAME OF THE LORD

Medieval castles were owned by a noble – a king, lord, knight or, occasionally, lady, who ruled the local area

Only **friends** and personal **servants** had contact with the lord and lady

Home from home

* Lords didn't necessarily live in one castle all the time. English kings and the very rich owned several castles.

* The lord's family would have private rooms or apartments in the keep that included a bedroom with an en-suite toilet, and a room where they entertained guests.

THE KING

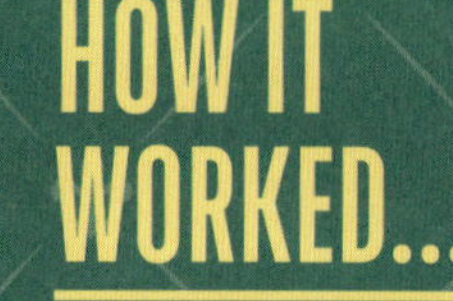

BARONS

THE CHURCH

HOW IT WORKED...

The Normans brought **feudalism** to England when they took over the country in 1066.

William the Conqueror kept about a fifth of the land for himself and shared the rest between loyal nobles (also known as barons) who, in return, paid him fees from the money they earned through rents and tax.

The Church was allowed to keep whatever land it had, but also paid fees to the crown.

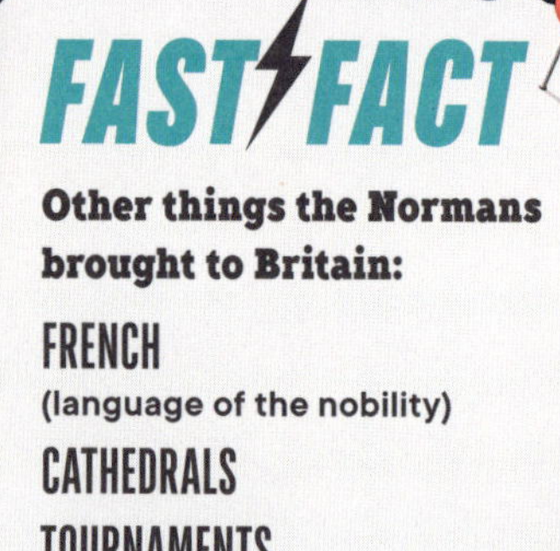

The Peasants' Revolt

Not surprisingly, there came a point in the 14th century when French peasants decided they'd had enough of this cruel and unfair feudal system. They rebelled and some castles were burnt down.

In 1381, England had its own Peasants' Revolt in protest against tax.

A castle owned by the King's uncle was destroyed as part of the uprising, and the peasants briefly took control of the kingdom's capital city, London.

After King Richard II (just 14 years old at the time) agreed to talk to the rebels he gave in to their demands, but their leader Wat Tyler was killed. The rebels went home, and sneaky Richard forgot all about the promises he made!

LAW & ORDER

In early medieval times, each lord was, in effect, the chief of police, judge and tax collector of the local area.

Criminals were kept in the castle keep while they waited to be sentenced or for a ransom to be paid. Prison as a punishment came in later.

By the 12th century the king had taken control of criminal justice, so nobles looked to make up for the money they no longer made from fines and taxes by taking jobs in the government.

THE HIERARCHY IN MEDIEVAL EUROPE

THE KING

Nobles needed the king's permission to build a castle.

BARONS

The king needed the support of nobles to maintain control of his kingdom, so he divided its territories between them.

KNIGHTS

These warriors on horseback were given special status and, sometimes, their own land in return for their loyalty to the king and his nobles.

FREEMEN

Some farmers made enough money to live off their own land. They were poor, but not controlled by the local lord.

PEASANTS

Ordinary folk farmed and lived on the local ruler's land. In return, they gave what they grew to the nobles and tried to get by on what was left.

SERFS

These people were even worse off than the peasants. They had no rights, were treated without respect and bought and sold by nobles like slaves.

Villein to villain!

Peasants were called villeins and seen as people not to be trusted. Over time, 'villein' became the modern word 'villain'.

FIRST LADIES

Little is known about how the wives of lords lived, apart from the fact that they sometimes played an important role in political power games...

UNFAIR, M'LORD!

Legally, the lady of the castle could own, inherit and sell land, but most women's lives were controlled by their father and husband.

✸ **Girls were thought ready for marriage at the age of 12 and usually married by 14.** They could be valuable to their family because a would-be husband may pay to marry them. There was no such thing as divorce.

✸ Once married, the wife received a **dower**. This was a gift of one third of the husband's land, but he could sell that without her permission!

✸ A lord's daughter was often brought up by another family in a different castle or a convent.

✸ **Needlework**, **music** and **reading** were usually among ladies' pastimes, but some enjoyed **hunting** and **chess** too.

An early 15th-century picture of women hunting

THEY RULED TOO

The lady of the castle looked after guests and kept them entertained, and was **in charge when the lord was away**.

Many ladies were **strong, capable** and **formidable women**. The wives of the English kings, William the Conqueror, Henry I and Henry II all **ruled the country** in their absence.

Eleanor's effigy on her tomb in the Royal Abbey of Our Lady of Fontevraud

Eleanor of Aquitaine

A French noble, Eleanor has been described as the **most powerful woman of the medieval era**.

✶ When her father, the Duke of Aquitaine, died in 1137, Eleanor, 15, inherited a huge fortune.

✶ The same year, she married King Louis VII of France. They had two daughters but no male heir, and the marriage ended in divorce.

✶ Eleanor went on to marry Henry of Anjou, who in 1154, took the English throne as Henry II. As a queen she was fearless, intervening in court politics and, in 1173, encouraging her sons to rebel against their father. An angry Henry locked her up in Salisbury Castle.

✶ After Henry died 16 years later in 1189, she was released and went from castle to castle in England and France as a VIP guest. She ruled on behalf of her son, Richard I (aka Richard the Lionheart), when he was away on a crusade.

✶ Eleanor was 82 when she died and was buried alongside Richard and Henry II at Fontevraud, in France's Loire valley.

KIDS IN THE CASTLE

What life was like for medieval children – rich and poor

RICH KIDS

Up until the age of 10, girls and boys wore dresses

Kids often slept on a bed on wheels called a truckle or a trundle. It was stored under their parents' bed

12 **14**

Girls could marry aged 12, boys had to wait until they were 14

The children of the rich sometimes wore jewellery

Girls usually had their long hair parted in the middle and tied in plaits

EDUCATION

Schools didn't officially exist, but posh kids were often sent away to be educated in another castle

✷ Lessons were usually taught by the castle's **chaplain** or one of his **clerks**.

✷ There was **no paper**. The medieval version of paper was vellum (stretched animal skin), but that was expensive. So, in lessons, pupils scratched on board covered in wax with a stick or a bone.

✷ Lessons would be **memorised** and then the boards would be smoothed over and used again.

Latin, the language of the Roman Empire, was taught to children and used by European nobles.

✷ **Other subjects** included Rhetoric (persuasive speaking), Logic, Arithmetic, Geometry, Astronomy and Music.

✷ **Girls** were taught needlework, singing, music and archery.

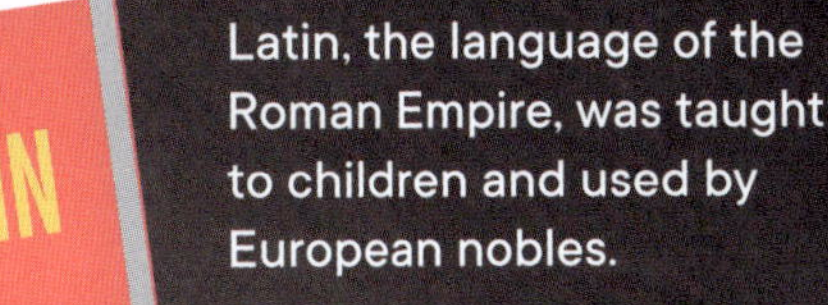
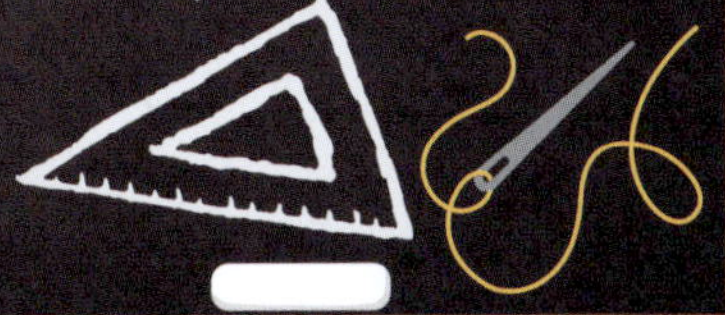

OTHER KIDS

There was no formal education for those children who lived in and around the castles but weren't from a noble family. Instead, they had jobs to do...

WORKING IN STABLES AND KENNELS

CARRYING WATER

GATHERING FRUIT AND NUTS

HERDING GEESE

PLANTING SEEDS

HARVESTING CROPS

MILKING COWS

ROASTING MEAT

HELPING KNIGHTS (as a Squire)

WORST OF ALL

Working for the gong farmer (that is, helping dispose of wee and poo!)

Toys

These included **dolls** (poorer children had **poppets**, dolls made from rags), little **pots** and **pans**, **toy knights** on horseback and **spinning tops**.

Games

✷ Noble boys enjoyed **hunting** and **shooting arrows** from bows.

✷ Other games included early versions of **leapfrog**, **blind man's buff**, **tag**, **hide-and-seek** and **tug-of-war**.

✷ In the game **Hot Cockles**, a player put on a blindfold and knelt down. Someone then hit that kneeling player, who then had to guess who had whacked him or her. This was not a complicated game!

KNIGHTS

Who were these warriors on horseback and why were they so important in medieval times?

LOYALTY SCHEME

During the early medieval period, knights lived in castles' garrisons

✹ They were the Lords' personal bodyguards who were rewarded for their loyalty and bravery.

✹ Later, some knights became so wealthy they no longer needed to fight for a living. Instead, they became **vassals** who paid a local lord **scutage**. This money was paid in exchange for being allowed to live on land awarded to them.

✹ These loyal subjects also pledged their life-long devotion to the local ruler.

✹ That pledge was made during an official ceremony, known as **homage**, that took place in the local castle's chapel or a cathedral.

BOYS TO MEN

BOYS (not girls – sorry!) could begin to train to become knights as young as seven years old.

PAGES They were known as pages until they turned 14 when they became squires to a knight.

SQUIRES cleaned the knights' armour and got them ready for battle. Sometimes they'd go into battle alongside their master.

KNIGHTS After years of training, **aged 21**, the squires became knights.

The Crusades

* Knighthood reached its peak during the religious wars known as the Crusades.

* These were waged by European Christian nations, from 1096 to 1291, in countries ruled by Muslims.

* Orders of knights from different nations fought as one international force.

BODY ARMOUR

CHAIN MAIL

☀ **From 1200 onwards** knights wore clothing made of small, linked metal rings.

☀ This was expensive and difficult to make and soon became rusty. One of the squires' jobs was to rub it with sand to get the rust off.

☀ Knights also wore a tunic on top and a helmet made from metal plates.

☀ Helmets had slits for seeing through and holes for breathing.

METAL PLATES

By 1350, knights were also wearing metal plates to protect the chest, arms, legs, hands and feet.

FULL METAL SUITS

☀ **From around 1450,** knights were covered from head to toe in metal plates. Helmets known as **armets** had a section on a hinge that could be lifted up when not in battle.

☀ Suits offered protection, but were heavy and difficult to get on and off.

☀ If dented, a blacksmith might be needed to free the knight from the wreckage!

SABATONS
protected feet

ARMET

MACE

WEAPONS

SWORD AND DAGGER

Every knight had these. They were kept in a case called a **scabbard**.

SHIELD Early shields covered the area from the knees to the chin and were made of wood or leather. Later, metal shields protected the area from the shoulder to the waist.

HAMMER

protected
hands

ON HORSEBACK

Knights used a lance. Shorter weapons were called **hafts**. These included the **mace**, the **war hammer** and the **battle axe**.

End of the knights

As the 14th and 15th centuries wore on…

✳ Soldiers on foot and bowmen found it easier to win battles against knights.

✳ Deadly gunpowder and artillery were introduced.

✳ Kings became more powerful, nobles and knights less powerful.

✳ By the 16th century, 'knight' was just the honorific title (status symbol) it is today.

The accolade

✳ The accolade is the medieval ceremony in which someone is made a knight.

✳ Several European countries have a version of the accolade. In the UK, when a man is awarded a knighthood, he kneels before the king or another member of the royal family, who touches the knight-elect's two shoulders with a sword.

✳ The British monarch still has 11 different knighthoods he can award.

✳ Women are made a Dame instead, and don't have an accolade – unfair!

Philosopher Sir Roger Scruton being knighted in 2016 by the then Prince of Wales

TRUSTY STEEDS

Horses were all-important to knights and a big part of castle life. They were the cars, trucks and tractors of the medieval age

WAR HORSE

A knight's war horse was known as a **steed** or a **destrier**

Long **stirrups** and a **saddle** with a high back and front meant the knight was, in effect, standing astride his steed!

With a sword in one hand and a shield in the other, a knight had to **control his horse** with his **legs** and **body**

Part of the knights' code of chivalry was that they must **never deliberately harm a steed**

SHAFFRON

A CURB BIT

Placed in the horse's mouth, this controlled the head

PEYTRAL

HORSE SHOE

Other castle horses

Horses were kept in the stalls of stables in the castle grounds, and because they were needed for so many tasks, there would be lots of them!

They wore leather harnesses and wooden saddles, and metal shoes made and fitted by a farrier.

Earning your spurs

SPURS

Riders wore metal **spurs** on their feet. They were dug into the horse to encourage it to go faster. Part of the ceremony to award a knighthood included giving the knight new spurs.

Full knight and horse armour in The Grand Armoury of Peles Castle, Romania

PROTECTION

❋ Horses were not protected for battle until the early 12th century. Even then they were just covered with a thick cloth!

❋ From around 1200 onwards, horses wore chainmail as well as protective pads of cloth and leather.

❋ Later, in the age of armoury, they wore metal protectors on the **chest** (a peytral), their **hind quarters** (a crupper) and the **head** (a shaffron).

TYPES & JOBS

Today we usually think of a horse being one of a breed, but in medieval times they were more likely to be identified by how they were used.

ROUNCEY Everyday horse used for transport and battles.

HOBBY Lightweight mounts used by cavalry.

PALFREY Taller, better bred and more expensive option for riding and hunting.

JENNET Another upmarket option, often ridden by ladies.

CHARGER Strong, fast and good for hunting and war.

DRAFT HORSE Also known as an affer or a stott, it was used for ploughing and transporting heavy loads.

WORK HORSE Pack horse (also known as a sumpter) or a cart horse.

HACKNEY Everyday riding horse sometimes used as a pack horse.

Sidesaddle, m'lady!

From around 1350 onwards, ladies sat on horses sideways on a special saddle. Others just rode around in horse-drawn coaches.

FAST FACTS

1. Castles were the **biggest** and **most important** buildings in the area and their owners were its **rulers**.

2. During the medieval period, only a **small number of very wealthy people** owned castles.

3. Most people **could not read or write** and lived and worked in the countryside where **life was hard**. A job in the local castle was a very **prized position**.

During the siege of 1216, Dover Castle was defended by **140 KNIGHTS & 1,000 SERGEANTS**

CASTELLAN

Also called a constable, this was a trusted official who was left in charge of the castle when its owner was away. He would usually have his own quarters away from his soldiers.

SOLDIERS

All castles needed soldiers to defend them. They lived within the castle walls in a building called a garrison, where they slept in a dormitory and ate together.

* Soldiers were in charge of security – opening the gate, lowering the drawbridge and patrolling the castle on the lookout for thieves and invaders.
* If a castle came under attack, the lord took in as many soldiers as possible to defend his territory.
* A battle-ready soldier was called a **sergeant**. Their commanding officer was the **castellan**.
* A **man-at-arms** was a high-ranking soldier or knight who was expert in using arms in battle.

SERVANTS

There were no fancy gadgets or electricity, so everything had to be done by hand, and castles had lots of servants to do just that.

An ordinary servant, such as a porter, **worked from sunrise to sunset** and was expected to **sleep in any quiet spot** they could find in the castle.

Days off were rare and **pay was poor**. Still, they might have a uniform in the lord's family colours (called livery) and **regular meals**.

PAGE

This boy servant sometimes went on to become a trainee knight, known as a squire.

BUTLER

Now thought of as a posh personal assistant, the word comes from the job title 'bottler', the person in charge of the wine in a medieval castle.

TRENCHERMAN

The servant who carried and served plates (trenchers) of food.

BARBER

Not only did barbers cut the lord's hair, they also did dental work – pulling teeth out with a pair of pliers being a speciality!

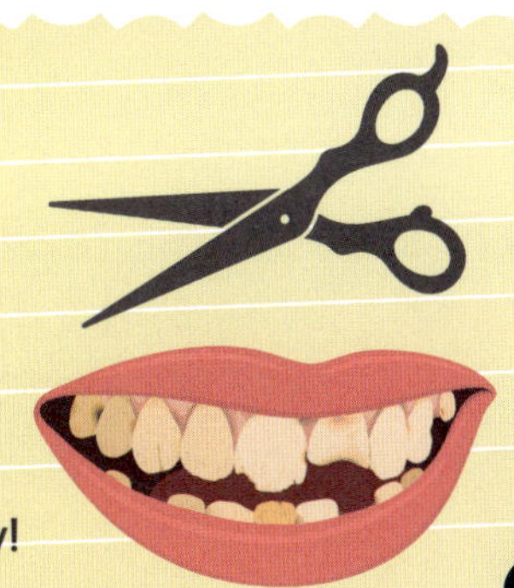

LADY-IN-WAITING

Also known as a damsel, this was an unmarried but well-born personal servant to the castle's noble women. There might have been several of them in m'lady's squad.

CHAPLAIN

The priest who looked after the castle's chapel. He **took daily mass** and, along with his clerks, was **often in charge of educating the nobles' children**.

CLERK

Some of the few people who could read and write were employed as clerks to **keep records of payments and laws**. They were often connected to the local church and worked under the chaplain.

SHERIFF

The lord's man who **collected rent or tax** from the peasants and applied laws was often based at the local castle.

CHAMBERLAIN

The trusted official **in charge of the household**, including the nobles' private rooms.

CARPENTER

Anything wooden from bowls to beds was made by the carpenter.

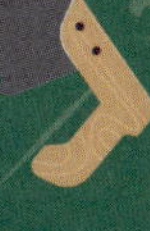

COOK

A cook might have to provide two meals for a couple of hundred people every day. Other household jobs included baker, brewer and laundress.

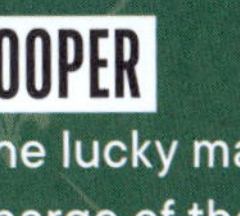

COOPER

The lucky man in charge of the barrels or casks where beer and wine were stored.

ARMOURER

The metalworker who made and repaired weapons and armour.

TANNER

A tanner made items from leather.
GROSS FACT ALERT!
Once the hair was removed from the animal skin the tanner would soften it by rubbing in dog or pigeon poo!

BLACKSMITH

Made nails, gates and anything else from iron and did repairs.

GRANGER

The person who looked after the grange or barn where grain was stored.

GONG FARMER

- In medieval times, loos and poos were both called gongs.

- A castle toilet or latrine was simply a wooden board with a hole in it. The toilet would hang over an outside wall, and poo would drop into the moat or a pit below.

- The lord had his own private loo, but everyone else would use one of a few gongs all in a line.

- People in medieval times didn't know about germs, but they believed bad smells caused illness.

- To stop the pong from drifting up into the castle, the pits would be cleaned out by the gong farmer.

Poo would be dumped into wheelbarrows or baskets and taken off to be buried or spread on fields as fertiliser.

It's said gong farmers were quite well paid, but people tended to avoid getting too close to them…

HOME COMFORTS

They may not have had iPhones and Deliveroo, but the Lord and Lady had a few things that made their castle deluxe and delightful

LIGHT

☀ As this was long before electricity, residents depended on a fireplace, flaming torches and tallow candles (made from animal fat) for light.

☀ Many castles had little shelves built into walls where a candlestick could be placed.

☀ Castles would go through hundreds of candles on a winter's night.

FURNITURE

☀ The very richest might have beds, but furniture, including chairs, was a rare luxury in medieval times.

☀ The most common item was a chest used to store clothes, books and valuables. When they travelled around, nobles took their chests with them.

* In early castles, the ground-level floor was made from earth, stone or plaster. Upper levels had timber floors.

* Later floors were made of cold, hard stone and dried rushes (a plant with strong stem-like leaves) were scattered over them.

* Among the rushes you might find beer dregs, spills of grease, bits of bone, spittle and dog and cat poo!

* Other floor coverings included mats made of rush, fur rugs and tiles. Carpets were put on walls, tables and benches, but not used on floors until the 14th century.

* Tapestries were sometimes used as dividers between rooms.

* Walls were whitewashed inside and out. Interior walls might also be plastered and have wood panels that were decorated with paintings or hangings, which also prevented draughts.

* One popular form of decoration was to whitewash the wall, outline its blocks of stone in red and paint a flower in each block.

* Henry III's walls were painted in his colours – green, gold and silver.

Passages

* There might be a passage to the kitchen, but generally rooms were connected or joined by staircases and there were no internal corridors.

* External passages, called **pentices**, might link buildings. They were covered, had windows and some even had their own fireplace!

* The chapel was arguably the most important place in the castle. By the 13th century, it was often located near the Great Hall.

* There were two levels to the chapel, the higher one for the Lord and family (naturally!), and the lower for everyone else.

* The castle's most expensive items were often in the chapel. These included the priest's fancy robes, and gold and silver plates and ornaments.

* Some chapels had a separate room where the nobles sat during a service, away from ordinary folk!

FAILED ATTEMPT

In 1238, a would-be assassin broke into Henry III's bedroom only to find the king had decided to sleep in the queen's bedroom that night. Bad luck!

Bedtime stories

* The Lord's bed had **curtains** that were closed at night for privacy and for protection from draughts.

* These beds could be taken apart and **transported** with the lord on visits to his other homes and castles.

* The bed frame was made of heavy wood, and **springs** were made of rope and strips of leather.

* The **mattress** was stuffed with feathers and beds also had sheets, pillows, quilts and covers made of animal fur.

BEDROOM

* The Lord and Lady's bedroom was known as a **solar**.

* The only other furniture would be chests and pegs (known as **perches**) for clothes, and a stool or two.

* Personal servants might also sleep in the chamber on a basic bed or a bench.

* Some of the bedrooms had **squints**, peepholes in the wall hidden in decorations, through which the Lord could see what was going on in his Great Hall.

* A small room or built-in wardrobe for dressing and dressmaking could be attached to the chamber.

* The Lord and Lady may also have **separate bedrooms**, with the Lady sharing with her companions, the ladies-in-waiting.

In the 13th century, small 'oriel' rooms were built by wealthier lords. These were attached to the chamber and were, like a modern sitting room or lounge, a private place for the family.

These were wooden and had a window and a fireplace. The 14th-century version was bigger and had a bay window.

Oriel window at Barnard Castle

BATH TIME

Only the wealthy had a bath. The very wealthy would have this drawn by their servant, the bathman.

✳ Baths were made of **wood**, lined with canvas and **moved around** so they could be taken by the fire in different rooms.

✳ These wooden tubs were protected by a tent or canopy. In warm weather, the tub might be placed in the garden.

✳ The Lord would take his bath (and the bathman!) with him when he went away.

✳ The more impressive 13th-century castles and palaces had permanent bathrooms. Henry III had hot and cold running water and Edward II had tiled floors and mats to keep his feet warm.

Toilets

Called latrines or garderobes, these were close to the chamber, but there were chamber pots under beds in case of emergencies during the night.

Magic touches

Some home furnishings were said to have special powers...

SEALSKIN was thought to have magic properties that could repel lightning.

A HARE'S FOOT tied to your left arm was supposed to keep you safe from danger.

THE BLOOD OF A LION was said to keep you safe from attacks from other animals.

SPRIGS OF ROSEMARY were attached to doors to ward off poisonous snakes.

SAGE left to rot with animal dung was thought to conjure up a bird with a serpent's tail...

A TYPICAL DAY

How lords, ladies and their servants went about their daily business

AT DAYBREAK...

Knights and men-at-war took over from the **nightwatchmen** in the towers and on the battlements.

Servants lit fires in the kitchen and the Great Hall.

Off to church

Mass in the castle's chapel, led by the chaplain, was a daily event.

Rise and shine

Lords and ladies woke up in their chamber. They usually slept naked and washed in cold water.

Breakfast

Pop Tarts had yet to be invented, so this was a simple meal of bread and wine or ale.

Hunting

* Some days, particularly during the summer, the lord might go hunting first thing in the morning and make breakfast a picnic in his forest.

* For the poor, hunting was just another way of finding food, but for nobles it was sport and military training.

* Castle owners would often also own an estate that included a forest where they, their rich friends and trained dogs could hunt boar, deer, foxes and stags.

* Falcons and hawks were also trained to kill smaller birds and animals. The **mew** was the building in the castle grounds where the hunting birds were kept.

Pastimes

If not hunting, the lord might discuss business with his steward and other senior servants, while the lady talked to guests or occupied herself with needlework or other hobbies.

Children would take lessons with the chaplain or one of his clerks or play with dolls, horseshoes, balls or bows and arrows.

Meanwhile...

The servants had their daily tasks. Domestic servants emptied basins and chamber pots and scattered fresh rushes on the floor, while many others were preparing lunch in the kitchen.

LUNCHTIME

Main meal

Between **10am and 12 noon**, the big meal of the day was served. This would have two or three courses, the last of which was nuts, cheese and fruit. Hands were then washed and the tables taken away.

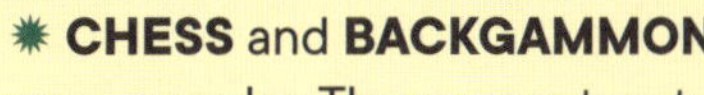

Fun & games

In the afternoon, it was time for the rich folk to relax and have fun!

✳ A **CAROLE** was a dance for which dancers joined hands and sang in a circle.

✳ **CHESS** and **BACKGAMMON** were popular. There were two types of chess, one similar to that we play today and the other, a simpler version played with dice.

Invented in India, chess spread to the Middle East where it was discovered by medieval Europeans during The Crusades (1095–1291).

EVENING

Supper

A supper was served in the late afternoon. This would be a light dish followed by cheese. Then it was time to relax in front of the fire. A late supper might also be eaten just before bedtime, which was usually quite early as they only had candles and fires to see in the dark.

Bedtime

Then it was time for the chamberlain to check the bedroom's basin and chamber pot were in place, help the lord out of his clothes and get ready for bed.

FOOD & DRINK

Eating and drinking were a **major part** of life in a medieval castle.

Not surprisingly, the **rich ate much better** food than the poor.

Many castles had **gardens**, **farms** and **fishponds** that supplied their food. Mushrooms and berries were collected from the **forest**.

There were **no fridges** so anything that might go off had to be eaten or drunk straight away.

BREAD

MOST IMPORTANT MEDIEVAL FOOD

✳ Wastrel was **white bread** made from finely sieved and ground grain for nobles.

✳ **Brown bread**, made from rye or bran, was eaten by the lower orders.

MEAT

✳ **Beef**, **mutton**, **duck**, **pheasants**, **swan** and even roasted **peacock** were eaten by the rich, but meat was generally too expensive for the poor.

BLOOD MONTH

November – when animals were slaughtered and their meat salted or smoked for the winter

✳ Roast peacocks were served with their feathers stuck back on!

✳ **Meat pies**, **pasties** and **fritters** were all on the menu.

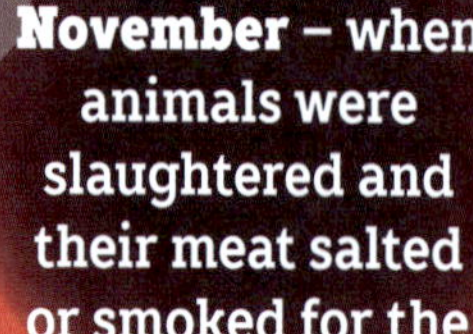
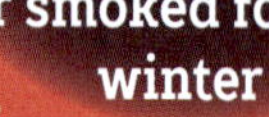

FISH

✳ In line with Christian tradition, fish was often eaten on Fridays. Favourites included **salted cod** and smoked or fresh **herring**.

Salty!

Meat, butter and fish were all salted to keep them fresh, particularly over the winter when food was scarce. The food was either buried in a pile of salt or soaked in salty water.

✳ **Sturgeon** and **whale** were rare delicacies said to be fit for royals.

✳ Much of the meat came from hunting in the lord's forestland.

* These were grown within the castle walls.

* They did not include **potatoes** – they weren't grown in Britain before the 18th century.

* **Onions**, **garlic**, **peas** and **beans** were the most common.

* Fruit picked from the castle orchard included **apples**, **pears**, **plums** and **peaches**.

PASS THE SAUCE!

Sauces were made of herbs, wine, verjuice (the juice of unripe grapes), vinegar, onions, ginger, pepper, saffron and cinnamon, all ground together. Mustard was also popular.

ADDED EXTRAS

* **Food dye**, such as the red of **sandalwood** and the green of **parsley** or **mint**, were used to make dishes look more attractive.

* **Herbs and spices** were ground and added to food. **Ginger was more expensive than gold** and, like other imported spices, only eaten by the rich.

* **Sugar** (including a type mixed with roses and violets) was rare and expensive, so **honey** was used to sweeten dishes.

* **Figs**, **dates**, **raisins**, **rice**, **almonds**, **oranges** and **pomegranates** were imported luxuries.

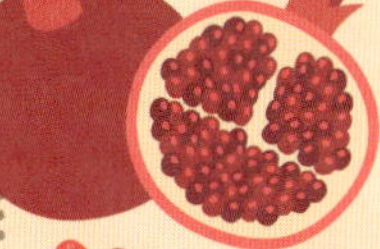

DRINK

WINE was for the **wealthy**

BEER AND MEAD (an alcoholic drink fermented from honey and water) were for the **poor**

During the 13th century, barrels of wine were usually shipped in from Bordeaux in France. It was sometimes sweetened or spiced, but went off within a year.

DID SOMEBODY SAY...
JUST EAT?

Time to get merry at the medieval castles' feasts

IT'S READY!

※ Feasts took place in the castle's Great Hall. Meals were announced with the blow of a horn. The diners would then wash their hands and say a prayer before tucking in.

※ The lord and his noble family sat separately from their guests at the high table on a dais (a raised platform).

※ A feast was a ceremony in which there was a set way of doing everything, including the order in which dishes were served and how they must be presented.

※ There was even a correct number of fingers with which a servant should hold a joint of meat while the lord carved it!

'TASTE THIS, WILL YOU?'

Some royals and top nobles had a **taster** who tried their food first in case it had been poisoned by an enemy

EXCUSE FINGERS!

※ Food was eaten with fingers or with a spoon after being cut up with the diners' own **personal knives** that they carried around with them. A big knife was used for cutting, and a smaller one was used for eating.

※ Plates were square platters called **trenchers** made from metal, wood or hard, stale bread!

5 RULES OF THE MEDIEVAL FEAST

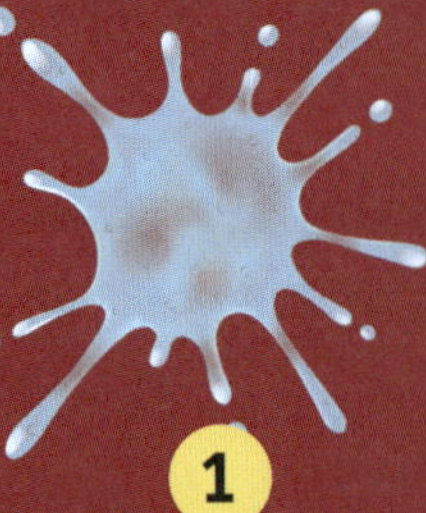

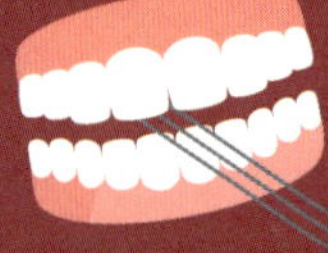

1 Do not **spit** on the table

2 Do not **burp** near another diner

3 Do not **pick your teeth** with a knife

4 Do not **scratch** your flea bites

5 Do not **fart**

FEAST DAYS

✳ Feasts were linked to ancient celebrations of agriculture and the Christian church.

✳ The biggest three took place at Christmas, Easter and Pentecost (or Whitsunday, the seventh Sunday after Easter).

✳ These feasts were followed by a week of holiday, at the end of which the castle had another feast!

WINTER

From Michaelmas (29 September) to Christmas when **rye** and **wheat** were sown

SPRING

Crops such as **oats**, **peas**, **beans** and **barley** were planted between Christmas and Easter.
At Easter, tenants would give the lord of the castle **eggs**, and in return he would give them dinner

SUMMER

This lasted from Easter to Lammas (1 August)

AUTUMN

Crops were harvested between Lammas and Michaelmas

A MEDIEVAL CHRISTMAS

✳ **The medieval Christmas holiday ran from Christmas Eve to the Twelfth Day (6 January).**

✳ **The lord of the castle gave gifts** of food, clothing, drink and firewood to his hayward, ploughman, shepherd, oxherd and swineherd to get them through the colder months.

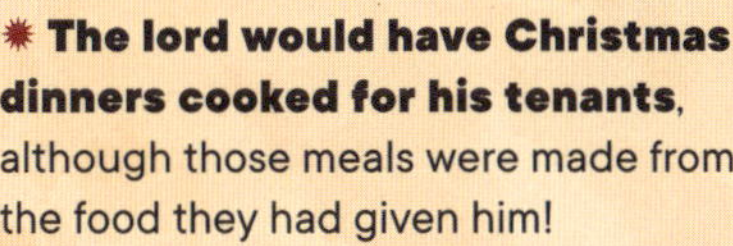

✳ **The lord would have Christmas dinners cooked for his tenants**, although those meals were made from the food they had given him!

✳ **Knights and senior servants were invited** to the castle's Christmas feast and given gifts of 'robes' (tunic, surcoat and mantle).

✳ A huge **Yule log** was brought in to be burnt on the Great Hall's fire throughout the 12 days.

✳ Lords would employ **extra watchmen** in case local people's celebrations got out of hand.

ENTERTAINMENT

✳ Diners were entertained by music, jokes and stories. A jester might put on a performance or a harpist would play.

✳ As well as the harp, musicians played the lute and the viele (which looked a bit like a violin).

✳ A guest might be invited to sing, and knights and lords were known to compose their own songs and poems.

CHEERS!

Drinks were drunk from metal, stone or leather goblets. The wealthiest had goblets made of gold or silver

WHAT THEY WORE

Lords and ladies of early medieval castles adopted distinctive but practical styles when it came to everyday clothes. Later, they got a little crazier with their hats, shoes, doublet and hose...

HEAD COVERINGS

✴ Indoors, the lord wore a linen cap or **coif** tied with string under the neck and the lady wore a linen **wimple**, a large piece of cloth that covered the head, neck and chin.

Outdoors, hoods and caps were worn over the coifs and wimples.

What's with the cone?

Perhaps the most famous medieval fashion item was the **cone-shaped hat** for ladies called the **hennin**.

The hat became popular in the mid-to-late-15th century, and some historians believe it was inspired by those worn by Mongolian noblewomen of the Ottoman empire.

It was made of a wire-mesh frame covered in fabric, with a veil, or cointoise, that hung down to the shoulders. Usually around 30–45cm high, a taller hat was considered by some to be a status symbol.

The hennin's popularity had faded by the time of the Tudors (1485–1603) who favoured a hooded headdress.

Escoffion

A lady's hat with two horns – and those horns could be up to a metre long!

Ladies arranged their **hair**, but styles were simple. Some wore **makeup** made of sheep fat to redden or whiten their skin

OUTERWEAR

Both sexes wore a long-sleeved **tunic**, fastened with a brooch, with a shorter sleeveless or wide-sleeved tunic called a **surcoat** on top. The surcoat was often lined with fur for warmth.

Both wore **belts** with a metal buckle. For special occasions they might be made of silk and adorned with silver or gold thread and jewels

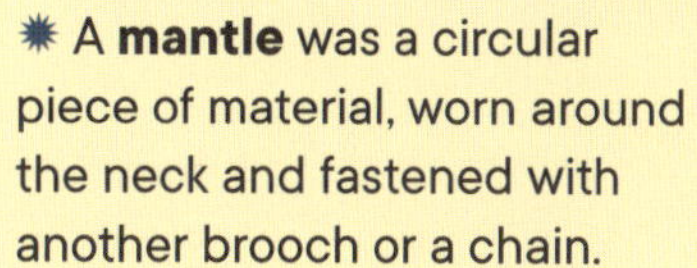

✳ A **mantle** was a circular piece of material, worn around the neck and fastened with another brooch or a chain.
Tunics and mantles were decorated with embroidery, tassels, feathers and ≠pearls.

✳ From around the mid-14th century, ladies wore the **houppelande**, a silk or velvet gown with long sleeves and a long train. Men also wore a version of the houppelande.

✳ The lord's garments were usually shorter and looser.
In the later medieval period, a **doublet** (short jacket) and **hose** (tights) became the thing to be seen in!
Sleeves and other parts of fancy 16th-century garments were sometimes **bombasted** – that is, stuffed with wool, horsehair, short linen fibres (tow) or bran to create different shapes.

MORE THIS WAY ▶

SHOES

✸ Lords and ladies wore **slippers** inside the castle and **low boots** or **pattens** (clogs that were worn over shoes), outdoors.

✸ In the late middle ages, men's shoes (sometimes called **poulaines**) with long toes were fashionable. The ends were filled with moss or whalebone and tied by string to the ankle to prevent the wearer tripping over them!

✸ Gloves were also worn and sometimes lined with fur.

UNDERWEAR & HOSE

✸ A lord also wore **hose** that was attached to his belt and held up his drawers (there was no elastic!).

✸ Linen (spun and woven from flax) was used for his lordship's **drawers** (also called braies) and the **chemise** (or kirtle) worn by his lady.

✸ Ladies wore **sock-length hose** held up with **garters** below the knee.

COLOURS

Clothes, hose and shoes were all in:

FABRICS

Wool and linen might be made locally but the rarer, more expensive fabrics came from abroad and were used and worn as status symbols. The most common fabrics were:

FURS

Only the rich could afford fur and the more animal skins used for an item of clothing the greater the status of its owner. They included:

JEWELLERY

Among the most obvious status symbols was jewellery. Rings in particular were prized, and used for seals (marks made in hot wax on important documents):

KNIGHT GAMES

Tournaments were a popular form of entertainment in and around medieval castles

TOURNAMENTS

These were made up of a series of contests between knights held at castles. They could go on for days with feasts in the evenings.

✳ Tournaments were entertainment, sport and training for knights.

✳ The lord of a castle had to be granted a royal permit to put on a tournament before he could challenge another noble and his knights.

The free tourney

There were two parts to this.
In the first, two teams of knights carrying lances on horseback charged at each other. For the second part, they battled with swords. This mock battle was called a **mêlée**.

WHAT IS JOUSTING?

In this contest, two knights on horseback, each carrying a long spear called a lance, galloped towards each other at top speed.

* The aim of the game was to knock your opponent off his horse.

* The **lances** used were **3.7 metres** or more long. They were often blunted to avoid serious injury, but jousting did sometimes lead to wounds and fatalities.

* The **winner** got to keep the **loser's horse and armour**. This was a bit of a money spinner, as they could be sold back to the vanquished for a tidy profit!

* The first record of jousting dates back to 1066 and it went on for hundreds of years. By the mid-17th century it had fallen out of fashion.

Two types of lance...

* **JOUST OF WAR** A lance with a sharpened end was used, and that could be lethal!

* **JOUST OF PEACE** Knights used a less dangerous lance with three or more prongs.

OH, HENRY!

Henry VIII had a go at jousting but gave it up after a **horse fell on him** during a tournament, leaving him with a serious leg injury.

Big prizes

The lady of the castle would often present the winners with prizes such as a gold shield, land, money or titles.

Tournament gear

* Competing knights would cover their helmets with a cloth called a **mantling** and top that off with a decoration called a crest.

* Special armour might be worn for particular events, such as a contest where knights fought on foot.

Foot combat

* For this contest, two knights in armour battled on foot. They were armed with swords or other handheld weapons.

* The knights' main aim was to **show off fighting skills** and overpower – **but not harm** – their opponent.

Medieval first aid

When knights broke bones they were reset using **plaster** and wounds were sealed with **egg whites**.

Old wine was used to stop wounds getting infected.

BADGE OF HONOUR

Heraldry was the way in which knights showed off their status and loyalty to a noble family

COAT OF ARMS

Each noble family had its own badge, known as a **coat of arms**, made up of a tincture (colour), ordinaries (shapes) and charges (symbols).

✳ Known as heraldry, badges were introduced in 12th-century England to distinguish one knight from another during tournaments, when helmets and visors covered faces and made recognition difficult.

✳ The badge would also be displayed on a knight's shield, surcoat, his horse's harness and banners.

✳ Knights spoke Norman French, and it's still used to describe coats of arms.

TINCTURE (colour)

There are nine common tinctures. The rule of tincture is that 'metal should not be placed upon metal, nor colour upon colour' so it stands out.

CHARGES (symbols)

✳ Each knight had a symbol on his shield on a coloured background.

✳ Its main emblem (or charge) was special to the family the knight represented. For example, if they owned farmland, the symbol might be a sheaf of wheat.

✳ Animals such as lions, leopards and dragons were used to symbolise bravery.

ORDINARIES (shapes)

There are said to be around 20 ordinaries and sub-ordinaries. They were sometimes combined, as in the cross and saltire of the Union Jack.

Heraldry had its own language. Many of the words have their roots in French. For example...

TINCTURES

OR
GOLD

ARGENT
SILVER

SABLE
BLACK

GULES
RED

ERMINE
representing the white fur with black tips of a stoat

VERT
GREEN

AZURE
BLUE

PURPURE
PURPLE

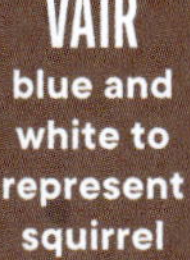
VAIR
blue and white to represent squirrel skin

TINCTURES

MULLET
Star

FLEUR DE LYS
Lily flower

ESCALLOP
Shell

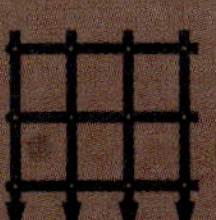
PORTCULLIS
Castle gate

GARB
Sheaf of wheat

MANCHE
Sleeve of a lady's dress

LION RAMPANT
Lion standing on its hind legs

LION PASSANT
Lion walking sideways

ORDINARIES

CROSS

CHIEF

BAR

SALTIRE

BEND

PILE

CHEVRON

FESS

PALE

UNDER SIEGE!

What happened when an enemy surrounded a medieval castle and trapped the lord, his family and their followers inside?

WAITING GAME

During the medieval period, sieges were more common than battles.

* Rulers preferred to avoid battles because they risked quickly losing men and land if things went wrong.

* If an enemy's attack on a castle was unsuccessful, they might camp outside, stop all supplies and wait until those inside surrendered.

* The attackers would sometimes set a deadline for surrender, after which the castle would be attacked.

* They might also dig ditches and put up fences around the outer wall, or build their own temporary siege castle from earth and wood.

SUPPLIES

How long those under siege could survive depended on the amount of food and water available.

* Large stores of grain to grind into flour for bread were essential.

* Krak des Chevaliers, the Crusaders' castle in the Middle East, had its own windmill on top of one of its towers to produce flour.

* Water could be stored in the castle's well and rainwater collected in large cisterns.

* Those trapped in the castle also had to deal with wounded soldiers and the spread of disease.

1 TUNNEL UNDER & BURN IT DOWN

Wooden fences and buildings are vulnerable to fire, but stone walls are difficult to set alight.

One tactic was to dig a tunnel with picks under a castle wall (usually under a tower or on a corner), prop the tunnel up with wood and then set fire to the timber to try and bring down the unstable wall.

This tactic was made more difficult if the castle's walls were built on natural rock or if its moat was full of water.

Before cannons, these underground mines were thought to be the most effective form of attack.

Bring on the pigs!

When King John laid siege to Rochester Castle in 1215, he ordered 40 fat pigs to be put in the mine his men had dug under the castle wall.

Once the timber inside was set ablaze, the lard in the pigs accelerated the fire and helped bring down the wall.

2 USE A BATTERING RAM

Soldiers used huge tree trunks to bash their way into the weaker castles. These rams were swung on leather straps and had a copper, iron or an actual ram's head (yes, really!) on the front end.

③ SHOOT!

Arrows were fired from bows at defenders of the castle and, from the 12th century onwards, bolts (or quarrels) were fired from crossbows. With a range of up to 365 metres, the crossbow was very useful to those under siege too. Catapults made from rope or hair were used to launch stones.

The ballista

This was simply a huge crossbow that fired extra-large bolts.

The trebuchet

First used by Italian armies in the late 12th century, a trebuchet was a huge catapult built with wood and used to fire stones of up to 250kg (that's the size of a fully grown lion!) in weight.

* **DEAD HORSES** and **RATS** were also sometimes flung into the castle in the hope they would spread disease!

* The trebuchet had a **LARGE HEAVY BOX** on one end of a long arm with the missile on the other end.

* To fire it, the heavy box was **DROPPED**, and the stone or diseased cow was **LAUNCHED** at and over the castle wall.

* This weapon was **EFFECTIVE** because it could hit the **SAME POINT** in the castle wall again and again until it was destroyed.

④ BRING YOUR OWN TOWER

Some brave soldiers might try to climb the castle walls using ladders, others used siege towers on wheels positioned near the walls. From there archers could fire arrows and soldiers could climb across bridges into the castle.

Moats were filled with soil, shrubs and trees from the forest so attackers could cross them.

Pits were dug and covered as traps to stop these towers being positioned at the foot of walls. Defenders would also try to set fire to the towers.

5 JUST BE PATIENT...

If a siege dragged on, starvation became an effective weapon. Castles would store up to a year's worth of supplies for that reason. Inside, the defenders would hold out as long as possible and eat horses, dogs, cats, rats and their leather belts if necessary!

If the castle was captured... the attackers might show the brave defenders due respect and let them march out unharmed – or they might just execute them!

Camping out

The attackers would have to bring all their own supplies and weapons to the castle and then camp out in tents until the siege ended.

Wealthy knights would, of course, bring their servants to look after them.

Desperate measures

In 1096, during the First Crusade, the Turks laid siege to western Christians in the castle of Xerigordos at Nicaea in modern-day Turkey.

The attackers cut off the castle's water supply and the defenders were forced to drink horses' blood and their own wee. Some were so desperate they buried themselves in damp soil in the hope that they would absorb some of its moisture.

SNEAKY!

Five cunning ways attackers got into medieval castles

1 **NIGHT-TIME ESCALADE** Climbing the walls under the cover of darkness.

2 **DIVERSION** Distracting a guard away from a gate.

3 **DISUSED WELL** or **LATRINE** Entering via a weak spot in defences.

4 **DISGUISE** Dressing as peasants or traders to gain entry.

5 **PLANT A SPY** This might be a soldier who pretended to switch sides.

END OF THE SIEGES

The motte-and-bailey castles of the 9th and 10th centuries were often under siege, but by the 11th century castles were more difficult to attack and invaders were not so keen.

Waging war to gain territories was outlawed in England by William the Conqueror, and the Crusades abroad became the priority when it came to conflicts. During the 12th and 13th centuries, castle sieges were rare.

CHAPTER 4

EXTRAORDINARY CASTLES

Inside some of the world's most famous and infamous fortified homes

WINDSOR CASTLE

Inside the oldest and largest occupied castle in the world

The Round Tower

Originally built in 1170, from the top, the view goes on for 25 kilometres on a clear day.

Disappointingly, the Round Tower is not actually round. One side was damaged in an attack during the 1200s. The tower was repaired, but left in a D-shape by Henry III. In the 1820s, George IV added around 10 metres to the top of the tower to make it look more gothic.

Since 1558, the tower's Norman Gate has been the home of the **Constable and Governor** who is in charge of the castle when the king is away.

THE LONG WALK

A path that connects the castle to the nearby Great Park, the trees that originally lined this **three-mile walk** were planted by Charles II in 1685.

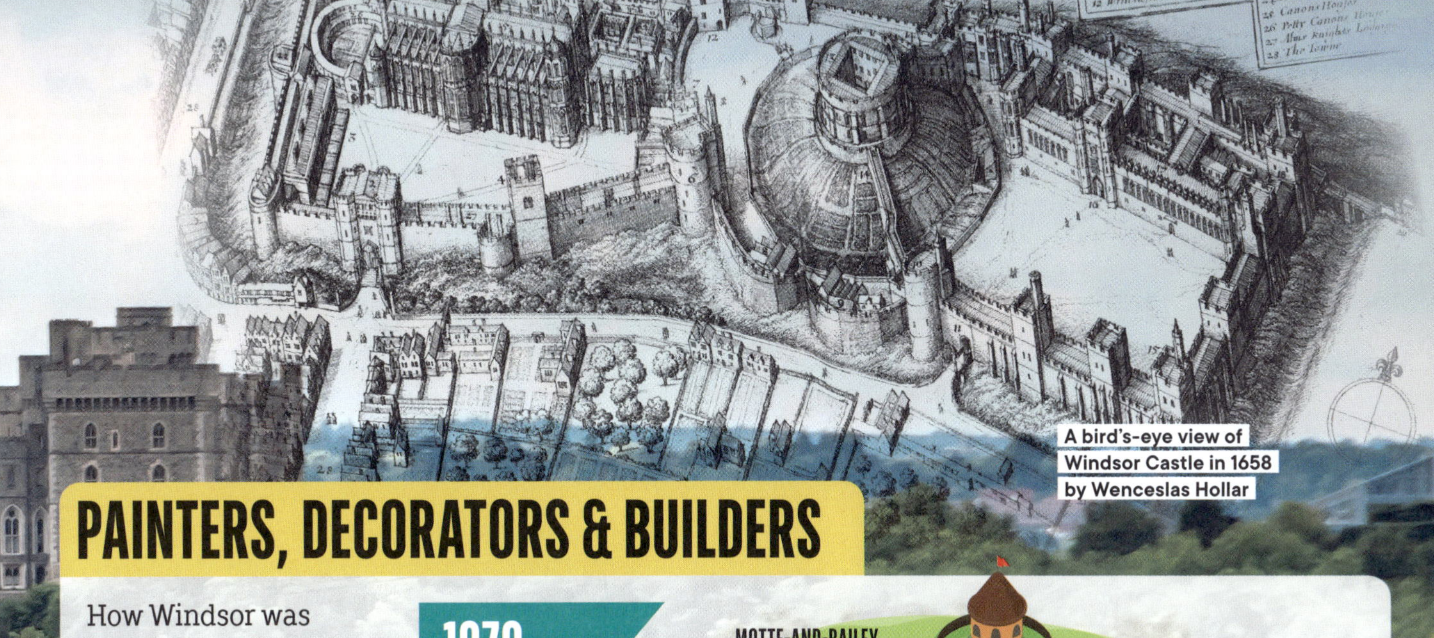

A bird's-eye view of Windsor Castle in 1658 by Wenceslas Hollar

PAINTERS, DECORATORS & BUILDERS

How Windsor was transformed from a military fortress into a stunning palace

800s

It's thought there was a royal residence of some kind on the site from the 9th century onwards.

1070

William the Conqueror begins building a wooden motte-and-bailey castle on the site, a hill overlooking the River Thames in the county of Berkshire. It takes 16 years to complete.

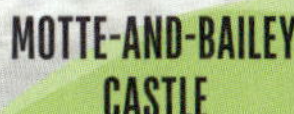

1154-1272

Henry II converts the castle into a palace with apartments and builds the stone Round Tower and stone walls. His grandson Henry III adds a chapel.

1350s-1377

King Edward III transforms Windsor into a gothic palace and builds separate apartments where the royal family can live and entertain.

The Norman Gate built by Edward III

1670s

Charles II creates new apartments, decorated with lavish tapestries, murals, carvings and painted ceilings in an attempt to rival his extravagant French cousin Louis XIV's Versailles.

1796-1820

George III makes the castle more medieval in appearance and makes Windsor the main royal palace.

1820s

George IV rebuilds the apartments as a place to host important visitors, adding a grand entrance and a staircase.

1837-1901

Queen Victoria adored Windsor and made it the place from where she ruled the British Empire.

Royal resting places

ST GEORGE'S CHAPEL Described as a gothic masterpiece, this chapel took over 50 years to build. Started during the reign of Edward IV in 1475, it was finished by Henry VIII in 1528.

Ten British monarchs are buried there including Henry VI, Edward IV, Henry VIII and his third wife Jane Seymour, Charles I, Elizabeth II, Edward VII and George V.

It was also the venue for Prince Harry and Meghan Markle's marriage in 2018.

ALBERT MEMORIAL CHAPEL Built by Henry VII and restored and renamed after her husband by Queen Victoria, this is the resting place of George III, George IV and William IV.

FROGMORE Queen Victoria and Prince Albert are buried in Frogmore, a mausoleum in Home Park near the castle.

FIRE!

In 1992, a fire broke out in Queen Victoria's private chapel. It was reported that a faulty spotlight set fire to a curtain next to the altar.

Flames spread quickly, destroying 115 rooms, including St George's Hall.

More than 200 firefighters fought the blaze for 15 hours with 5.7 million litres of water.

Miraculously, just two pieces of the castle's vast art collection were lost – a rosewood sideboard and a painting by Sir William Beechey.

By 1997, the castle was fully restored. The work cost £36 million, part of which came from opening Buckingham Palace to the public for the first time.

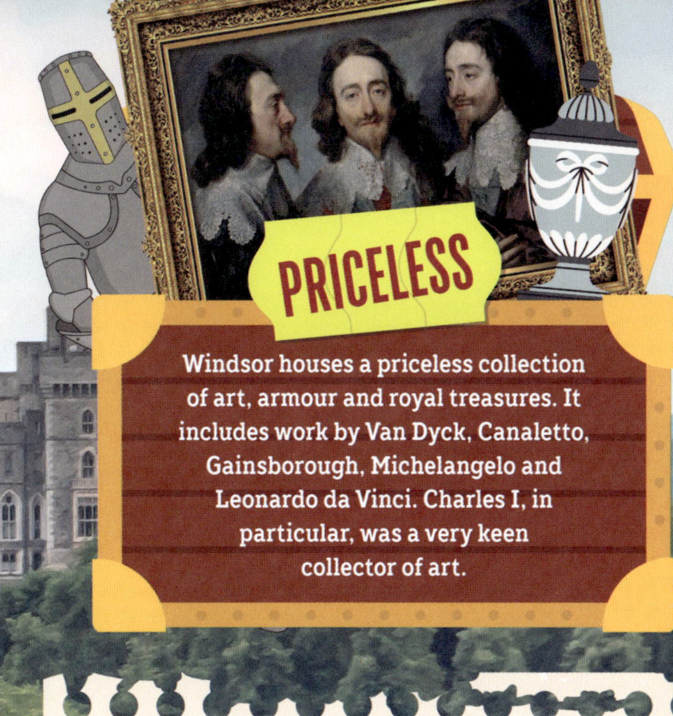

Windsor houses a priceless collection of art, armour and royal treasures. It includes work by Van Dyck, Canaletto, Gainsborough, Michelangelo and Leonardo da Vinci. Charles I, in particular, was a very keen collector of art.

Windsor today

The castle remains both a tourist attraction and a working palace.

King Charles III often spends weekends there, and the castle is still used for official state events.

They include **The Garter Ceremony** that celebrates the kingdom's oldest and most senior order of knights, the Order of Chivalry. New members of the order, founded in 1348, are installed at the ceremony which takes place every year in June.

As at other British royal palaces, a flag is flown when the king is in residence.

Your royal invitation

Windsor Castle is open to visitors for most of the year. You can tour the State Apartments and watch the **Changing of the Guard**, a ceremony in which one group from the British Army's Household Division take over duties from another. 'The Guards' have guarded the palace since 1660.

You can also pay a visit to **Queen Mary's Dolls' House**. It was built between 1921 and 1924 for Queen Mary, wife of George V, by Sir Edwin Lutyens, said to be the greatest architect of his day. More than 1,500 artists, craftspeople and manufacturers contributed to the dolls' house's construction. It has electricity, running water and working lifts.

Before World War II

The original castle was built sometime during the 11th century and rebuilt after it was destroyed by invading Hussites in 1430.

In the 18th century, it was converted into a workhouse and in the 19th century it became a hospital for the mentally ill.

ESCAPE FROM COLDITZ!

During World War II, Colditz Castle in Germany was a maximum-security prison where the Nazis jailed the Allied officers most likely to escape – not that it stopped them from trying...

STONE WALLS

2 METRES THICK
AT THE BASE

640KM
FROM ALLIED TERRITORY

'ESCAPE-PROOF'

❋ Colditz was made a prisoner-of-war camp at the start of World War II in 1939 and turned into a maximum-security prison the following year. The Nazis called it Oflag IV-C and said it was **'escape proof'**.

❋ Between 1941 and 1945, **1,500 prisoners of war** (POWs) from Britain, France, Belgium, the Netherlands and Poland were held in **700 rooms**.

❋ The castle is on a hill overlooking the Mulde River that flows through the town of Colditz in Saxony.

176 prisoners tried to escape

130 successful POW escape attempts were made

32 prisoners completed a 'home run' – that is they escaped and were not recaptured

POWs in the castle's courtyard

ESCAPE ATTEMPTS

As part of the war effort, British officers were expected to try to escape. Here's how they and others tried to break free…

HID IN STRAW MATTRESSES to be dumped outside the prison.

HID IN A PILE OF RUBBISH under a blanket with used cans and cardboard sewn onto it.

MADE ROPES from bedsheets and used them to climb out of windows.

CRAWLED THROUGH DRAINS and lifted their covers outside the prison.

DUG TUNNELS and hid the earth they removed in the castle's attic.

MADE CLOTHES AND UNIFORMS so they could pose as civilians and Nazi officers.

FORGED PAPERWORK to show to officials after making an escape.

MADE LIFE-SIZE DUMMIES to fool the Nazis into thinking all prisoners were accounted for.

Dutch Lieutenant Leo de Hartog with 'Moritz', one of the dummies POWs used to trick Nazi guards

French Lieutenant **Chasseur Alpin Bouley** tried to walk out of Colditz **disguised as a German woman**

Giles Romilly, nephew of Britain's wartime Prime Minister **Winston Churchill**, was an inmate at Colditz. Romilly escaped while being moved to another prison

A replica of the Colditz Cock glider in the attic of Colditz Castle

Delayed flight home

Ambitious POWs built a secret workshop in the castle's attic where they made the **Colditz Cock**, a glider with a 9.75m wingspan.

They worked on it for eight months, using floorboards, bits of beds and electrical wire from unused parts of the prison. Prisoners' sleeping bags were used for the glider's skin. The plan was to catapult the aircraft via a system that involved dropping a bathtub full of concrete from five floors up. The glider would then fly POWs over the prison walls.

The finished glider was never launched because the allies thought the Nazis might see it as an escape attempt too far and execute the POWs!

FREEDOM FOR ALL!
The US army took over Colditz and liberated its POWs in April 1945

Where is DRACULA'S CASTLE?

CASTLE BRAN
ROMANIA

Author Bram Stoker describes Dracula's castle as being in Transylvania (a region in modern-day Romania), on a rock above a valley with a flowing river below. Because it is the only castle in the area that matches his description, Castle Bran, built in 1377, is often taken to be the place the vampire's home was based on. Stoker never visited Romania, but it's believed he read about Bran and saw drawings of it.

Also, there is no doubt the writer was inspired by the stories of notorious dictator Vlad the Impaler, who was at large in the area during the 15th century (see Corvin Castle for further details…).

The dark prince's nickname was Vlad Dracula. Some have suggested that Vlad was not just an inspiration for Dracula, but that he was the blood-sucking vampire…

CORVIN CASTLE
ROMANIA

Also known as Hunyadi Castle, Corvin was built in 1440 as a fortress and a prison.

It's thought that Vlad Tepes, the 15th-century prince of Walachia in modern-day Romania – now best known as Vlad the Impaler – was held in its dungeon. This experience is said to have made Vlad so mad that it left him even keener to inflict pain on his enemies…

Vlad's ghost (a big guy in a tall hat) has been seen in the Knight's Hall near the entrance to the dungeon of this Transylvanian castle.

There is no evidence that Stoker was thinking of Corvin when he wrote *Dracula*, but it's often linked with the book. Screen versions have been filmed there including the 2024 movie, *Nosferatu*.

SLAINS CASTLE
SCOTLAND

Stoker wrote some of *Dracula* while visiting the village of Cruden Bay on the east coast of Scotland.

It's been said that the nearby Slains Castle is similar to Dracula's ancestral home as described in the book.

For example, both Slains and Castle Dracula have a central eight-sided windowless room.

Built around 1597 by Francis Hay, the 9th Earl of Erroll, the castle is now a ruin, but in Stoker's day it was still in the Earl's family and in use.

Winston Churchill and the writers Samuel Johnson, Sir Walter Scott and Robert Burns were all visitors.

Stoker uses Slains as a location for several other stories but, annoyingly, never confirmed it was the castle in *Dracula*.

The ruins of Slains' octagonal room

The book

The novel *Dracula* was written in 1897 by the Irish writer **Bram Stoker**.

One of the world's most famous stories, it has inspired hundreds of adaptations, in print and on screen.

In the book, Stoker tells us the vampire lives in Transylvania, in the country now known as Romania, but he never says exactly where Dracula's castle is, and there is no record of his real-life inspiration.

Another contender...?

Bram Stoker was a London theatre manager and wrote *Dracula* in his spare time. Before that he worked as a civil servant for ten years at **Dublin Castle** in the Republic of Ireland.

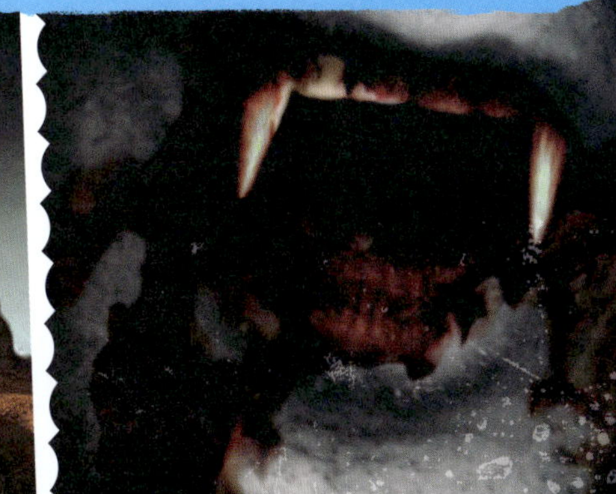

MOST HAUNTED!

Ghosts love a castle and these are some of the spookiest...

The queen, the king & the horseman

HEVER CASTLE KENT, UK

Built in the late 14th century, during the 15th and 16th centuries, Hever was home to the Boleyn family

Anne Boleyn, the second of Henry VIII's six wives, was born and raised at Hever Castle. After she failed to give birth to a male heir Anne was accused of treason and adultery and then executed. The famously horrible Henry later gave Hever to his fourth wife, Anne of Cleeves.

● **The ghost of Anne Boleyn** has been spotted in the gardens of the castle, where she was seen hammering on a window and scratching the walls....

● **Henry's ghost** was observed sitting in a bedroom where he is said to have slept....

● **A ghostly tall man on a horse** has been seen charging up and down Hever Castle's Long Gallery....

CHILLINGHAM CASTLE NORTHUMBERLAND, UK

Home to a host of ghosts, 13th-century Chillingham claims to be the most haunted castle in Britain

When a footman was locked in the castle's pantry overnight to guard the family silver, he saw The White Pantry Ghost, a female apparition who begged him for water. It's said this was the ghost of a victim of poisoning.

● Also, during restoration work, the bones of a child were found in the wall of a bedroom. These were thought to be the remains of 'Radiant Boy' or **'Blue Boy'**, a ghost said to haunt that room.

● Meanwhile, in the chapel, two **male voices** are often heard but never traced, a 'creeping sensation' has been felt in one of the rooms and there have been numerous sightings of **mysterious figures** in the courtyard.

The most haunted castle in Britain...?

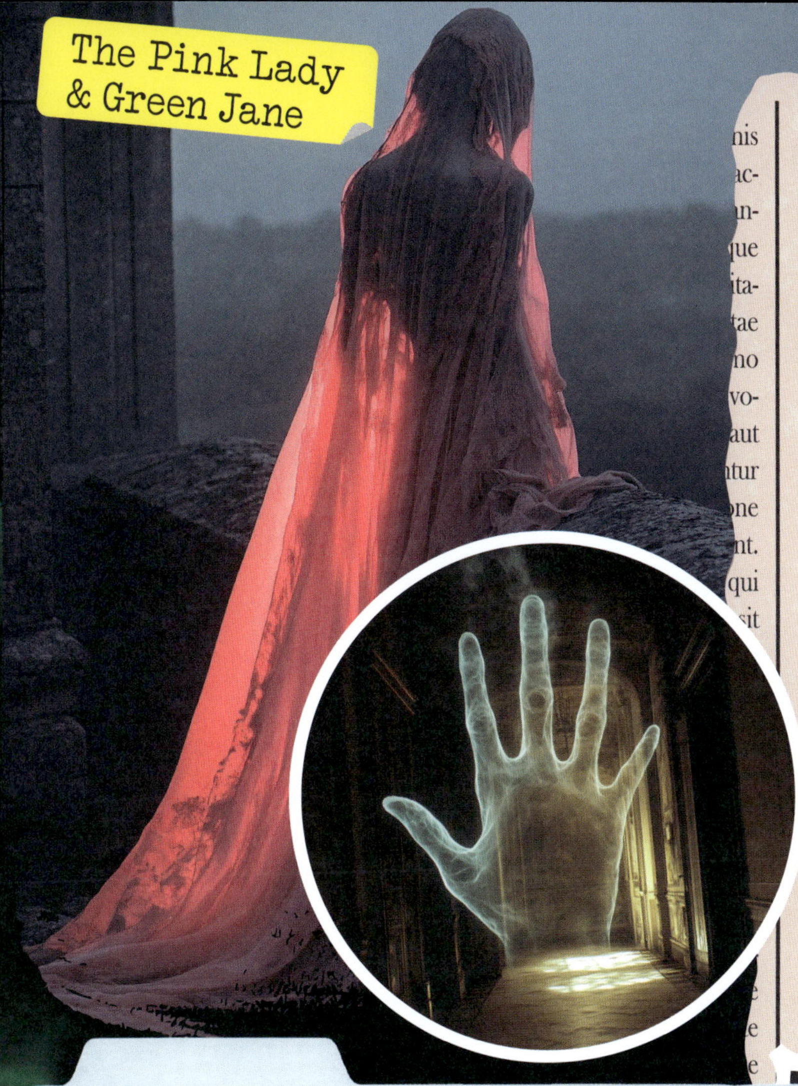

BAMBURGH CASTLE
NORTHUMBERLAND, UK

Every seven years, the ghost of a heartbroken princess is said to move through this castle's corridors

The Pink Lady is said to have thrown herself from the battlements after her father, the king, sent away her lover for seven years. The king bought her a pink dress to cheer her up. It didn't work. Obviously.

🟢 The ghost of a **young man** who took his own life there during World War II, when it was used as a rest home, is said to sit at the bottom of a staircase.

🟢 A ghost has been seen near the clock tower, carrying a bundle under her green cloak. This is **Green Jane**, who, as she held her baby, was pushed down steps and died after she asked castle guards for help.

🟢 In the 18th century, **Dr John Sharp** restored the castle. Now he's said to haunt it, refusing to leave his beloved home…

LEAP CASTLE COOLDERRY, REPUBLIC OF IRELAND

Strange apparitions make Leap, built between the 13th and 15th centuries, the creepiest of Irish castles

One of the many ghosts that haunt Leap is that of a priest killed by his brother in The Bloody Chapel. A mysterious light has been seen shining from the chapel windows at night.

🟢 In the Main Hall, **two girl ghosts** have been seen. One is thought to be **Emily** who died after falling from the battlements. The other is **Charlotte**, her sister, who had a deformed leg. The ghost of their **governess** is said to sometimes appear with them.

🟢 An invisible apparition called **The elemental** has been felt by some visitors.

🟢 Some say the trouble started after the castle was built on a site used by **druids** for sacred ceremonies…

BHANGARH FORT RAJASTHAN, INDIA

This 16th-century fort counts as a castle; it was built by Raja Bhagwant Das the ruler of Amber, for his son

According to folklore, a sadhu (priest) cursed the castle after the Raja broke a promise that it would not cast a shadow on his nearby home.

● The castle is said to be the most **haunted** place in India and tourists are not allowed to enter after sunset. **Voices** and **strange noises** are heard after dark, the site is full of bats and locals believe anyone who visits at night will not come out alive!

MOOSHAM CASTLE
SALZBURG, AUSTRIA

During witch trials of the late 17th century, this castle was where those found guilty were jailed, tortured and executed

Decades later, in the 1800s, so many deer and cattle were found dead in the castle grounds that residents were accused of being werewolves and killed!

● Visitors now often say they hear **banging sounds**, see **footprints** and **strange white mist** and feel someone or something **breathing on them** as they move around the castle.

HIMEJI CASTLE HIMEJI CITY, JAPAN

Built in the 14th century, Himeji Castle is Japan's largest and most visited castle

According to one version of a famous legend, after being wrongly accused of losing one of ten valuable dishes, the servant Okiku was killed and her body thrown in the castle's well.

● Her ghost is said to appear at night and can be heard **counting dishes**. When Okiku reaches dish number nine, she **howls in frustration** and returns to the well...

BURG ELTZ WIERSCHEM, GERMANY

Don't be fooled by the fairy-tale exterior, inside this 12th-century castle roams the ghost of Agnes, daughter of the 15th Count of Eltz

After Agnes rejected his advances, the Knight of Braunsberg attacked her family's castle. So Agnes put on her brother's armour and joined the fight to defend her home. Not knowing who she was, the rampaging Braunsberg killed her!

● It's now said **Agnes haunts her bedroom** where the armour she died in is on display. There have also been sightings of a **ghostly knight on horseback** at the castle gate. Could this be Braunsberg asking for forgiveness? It should be!

A 21ˢᵗ CENTURY MEDIEVAL

Why people are slowly constructing a 13th-century castle in the French countryside

UNFINISHED MASTERPIECE

In 1995, three friends and residents of the area decided to build Guédelon Castle from scratch the old-fashioned way at Treigny in France's Burgundy region.

✳ They considered rebuilding Saint-Fargeau Castle in that area, but decided to build a new medieval castle instead.

✳ They bought 27 acres of forestland and, in 1997, work began in a disused sandstone quarry.

✳ The friends were all history buffs and nature lovers and decided to build their castle exactly as it would have been built centuries ago.

✳ Guédelon is now run by a committee of archaeologists, historians and castle experts. It's been described as 'experimental archaeology' in which people are 'building to discover'.

✳ Research for the project is done in local castles and taken from old manuscripts and books.

✳ Six turrets, a protective wall, the interior of the castle and a chapel have all been completed, but it's estimated Guédelon could take up to 20 more years to finish – but that's not necessarily a bad thing...

Guédelon Castle's treadmill crane

A mason carves stone the traditional way

RESCUERS

Craftspeople from Guédelon worked on the reconstruction of the world-famous **Notre-Dame Cathedral** in Paris, after a fire in 2019 caused significant damage

ADVENTURE

NO CHEATING!

One of the main aims of the project is to pass on skills and knowledge.

* All work on the castle is done using medieval techniques, tools and materials. So that means no power tools, trucks or cranes.

* Local wood is used for construction and as fuel for fires. There are nearby and natural supplies of sand for mortar, clay for the roof tiles and ceramics, and the ochre used to colour them. All tools and nails are made in the castle's blacksmith shop.

* Guédelon has 70 members of staff and around 300,000 visitors a year. Tourists and groups of schoolchildren visit the site and see working craftspeople trained in heritage skills such as masonry, blacksmithing, carpentry, dyeing and animal husbandry.

* Workers dress in medieval clothing when possible (modern regulations mean they must wear sturdy boots and hard-hats).

* In the castle garden, only plants local to the area in medieval times are grown. They also have their own sheep for wool and geese wander the grounds.

Workers in medieval costume making rope

A beautifully crafted arrow loop

GLOSSARY

ARROW LOOP
Narrow vertical opening in a castle wall from where arrows can be fired.

BAILEY
Courtyard between the motte and the palisade.

BARBICAN
A fortified gateway.

BASTION
Extended section of a castle's wall from where a cannon could be fired.

BATTLEMENT
Gap at the top of a castle wall formed by crenels and merlons.

CASTLE
Fortified building that is home to a ruler, his family and followers.

CONCENTRIC CASTLE
Castle with several walls as layers of defence.

CRENEL
The gap or indentation of the battlement.

CRENELLATED
Built with a series of battlements.

CURTAIN WALL
Thick stone wall built around the keep.

DEVICE
Word used for Henry VIII's plan.

DOUBLET
A short jacket.

DRAWBRIDGE
Bridge over the castle's moat that leads to the gatehouse that can be drawn up to provide extra protection.

ESCOFFION
A lady's hat with two horns.

FEUDALISM
System by which royals used the rich to maintain control of the poor, and rule a country.

FORT
Building occupied by soldiers.

GARRISON
Building within a castle occupied by soldiers.

GATEHOUSE
Building located at the castle gate.

GONG FARMER
Servant who cleans out pits and moats of poo.

GREAT HALL
Main room in the keep used for feasts and entertainment.

HENNIN
Cone-shaped hat for ladies.

JOUST
A contest between two knights with lances on horseback.

KEEP
Castle's central tower where the ruler and family live.

MACHICOLATION
Gap in the wall that hangs over the side of the castle through which stones and boiling water were dropped on enemies. Also known as a 'murder hole'.

MEAD
Alcoholic drink fermented from honey and water.

MEDIEVAL TIMES
Period between 5th and 15th centuries, sometimes called the Middle Ages.

MERLON
The upright section either side of a crenel.

MOAT
Ditch that surrounds a castle.

MORTAR
Mix of chalk and limestone that holds together stones used to build a castle.

MOTTE
Mound on which a keep was sometimes built.

NORMANS
Castle-building people from what's now northern France who conquered England in 1066.

PALISADE
Wooden fence that surrounds early versions of castles.

PARAPET
Crenellated low stone wall.

PEASANT
Ordinary person who lives, works and rents land and a home on a ruler's land.

PORTCULLIS
Heavy grate that is a layer of protection at the castle's gateway.

SERF
Poor person bought and sold like a slave during medieval times.

SQUIRE
A knight's personal servant.

TREBUCHET
Huge catapult on wheels.

TURRET
Tower with a small room at the top from where approaching enemies can be seen.

INDEX

A
Arrow loop
22, 26, 93

B
Bailey
14, 17, 32, 77, 81

Battlement
23, 26, 28, 37, 60, 89

C
Crusades
16, 17, 47, 61, 72, 77

D
Device fort
18, 19

Dracula
86, 87

F
Feasting
7, 62, 64, 65

Fort
6, 7, 8, 9, 10, 18, 19

G
Gong farmer
45, 54

Great Hall
15, 17, 32, 34, 58, 60, 64, 65

H
Henry VIII
18, 19, 71, 88

Heraldry
72, 73

K
Keep
7, 11, 13, 14, 15, 17, 22, 24, 25, 32, 40, 41

Knight
13, 40, 41, 45, 46, 47, 48, 49, 50, 51, 53, 60, 65, 70, 71, 72, 77, 83, 91

L
Lady
32, 42, 51, 54, 56, 58, 60, 66, 67, 68, 71

Lord
14, 32, 40, 42, 46, 56, 58, 59, 60, 61, 62, 64, 65, 66, 67, 68, 70, 74

M
Merlin
10, 11

Moat
16, 27, 30, 75, 76, 93

Motte
14, 24, 77, 81

N
Normans
7, 12, 13, 24, 27, 40, 72

P
Parapet
15, 18, 25

Portcullis
27, 73

R
Romans
7, 8, 9, 10, 11, 15, 45

S
Servant
34, 37, 40, 46, 53, 54, 58, 59, 60, 61, 65

Siege
24, 25, 52, 74, 75, 76, 77

W
William the Conqueror
12, 40, 43, 77, 81

First published 2025 by Button Books, an imprint of Guild of Master Craftsman Publications Ltd, Castle Place, 166 High Street, Lewes, East Sussex, BN7 1XU, UK. Copyright in the Work © GMC Publications Ltd, 2025. ISBN 9781787081901. Distributed by Publishers Group West in the United States. All rights reserved. No part of this publication may be reproduced, stored in a retrieval system, or transmitted in any form or by any means without the prior permission of the publisher and copyright owner. While every effort has been made to obtain permission from the copyright holders for all material used in this book, the publishers will be pleased to hear from anyone who has not been appropriately acknowledged and to make the correction in future reprints. The publishers and authors can accept no legal responsibility for any consequences arising from the application of information, advice, or instructions given in this publication. A catalogue record for this book is available from the British Library. Editorial: Robert Hiley, Susie Duff, Jane Roe, Anne Guillot. Design: Tim Lambert, Klaudia Wolinska. Publisher: Jonathan Grogan. Production: Jim Bulley. Photos/illustrations: Michelle Urra, Sara Thielker, Alex Bailey, Shutterstock.com. Colour origination by GMC Reprographics. Printed and bound in China.